D1534250

THE

Myth of the

Resurrection

AND OTHER ESSAYS

Joseph McCabe

Prometheus Books • Buffalo, New York

Published 1993 by Prometheus Books

59 John Glenn Drive, Buffalo, New York 14228,
716-837-2475. FAX: 716-835-6901.

Library of Congress Cataloging-in-Publication Data

McCabe, Joseph, 1867–1955.
      The myth of the Resurrection and other essays / Joseph
McCabe.
              p.   cm. — (The Freethought Library)
      Originally published under titles: The Myth of the
resurrection. 1925. Did Jesus ever live? 1926. How Christianity
"triumphed." 1926.
      ISBN 0-87975-833-3 (pbk.)
      1. Christianity—Controversial literature. 2. Jesus Christ—
Rationalistic interpretations. 3. Free thought. I. Title.
II. Series.
BL2730.M33   1993
270.1—dc20   92-46038
                                                                    CIP

Printed in the United States of America on acid-free paper.

Additional Titles in
The Freethought Library

Debates on the Meaning of Life,
Evolution, and Spiritualism
Frank Harris, Percy Ward, George McCready Price,
Joseph McCabe, and Sir Arthur Conan Doyle

The Necessity of Atheism and Other Essays
Percy Bysshe Shelley

JOSEPH MARTIN MCCABE was born on November 11, 1867, of a Catholic working class family in Macclesfield, England. At the age of sixteen, Joseph entered the Franciscan seminary; upon his ordination at twenty-three, Joseph—now Father Anthony—was appointed to teach philosophy. However, the young priest began increasingly to doubt the truth of the Catholic religion. Finally, after weighing the evidence for and against belief in God and immortality and finding his faith "bankrupt," McCabe promptly abandoned both the priesthood and Catholicism.

Through the offices of his friend Sir Leslie Stephen, McCabe began a prodigious writing career, beginning with his autobiographical *Twelve Years in a Monastery* (1897). Following the success of this work, McCabe turned to biographies and translations. His translation in 1902 of Ernst Haeckel's *The Riddle of the Universe* spread McCabe's reputation throughout the English-speaking world.

Influenced by Haeckel's defense of organic evolution and its ramifications for science, philosophy, and theology, McCabe applied this same evolutionary view to the study of history: History, he argued, was to be regarded not merely as a record of events but as a scientific understanding of the development of human culture and social institutions. Human history, therefore, in line with the deterministic materialism of Karl Marx, was moving away from religion and oppressive monarchies and toward science and social equality, which would culminate in an enlightened new age. The threat to human progress, however, lay in the Church and its alliance with the bourgeoisie. McCabe saw this as a lethal union responsible for fascism in Europe and an assault upon communism and socialism, which McCabe regarded as harbingers of his new world order.

While in the earlier part of this century McCabe was

on friendly terms with the leading skeptics in English intellectual and political life, his aggressive candor and fractiousness led to his increasing isolation, the breakup of his marriage in 1925, and, in 1928, to his expulsion from the British Rationalist Association. From the late 1920s until his death, McCabe wrote almost exclusively for E. Haldeman-Julius, who—touting McCabe as "the world's greatest scholar"—published his work in 121 Little Blue Books and 122 larger volumes, which caustically inveighed against the evils and follies of organized religion and capitalism.

Despite misfortunes in his personal life, McCabe remained an optimist and an unflinching foe of "bishops, preachers, exploiters of the poor, millionaires, parasites, dictators, and liars and crooks generally." Joseph McCabe died, in his eighty-eighth year, on January 10, 1955.

McCabe's other published works include *The Story of Religious Controversy* (1929), *The Rise and Fall of the Gods* (1930), *Eighty Years a Rebel* (1947), and *The Papacy in Politics Today* (1937, 1943, 1951).

Contents

How Christianity "Triumphed"

The Myth of the Resurrection

1

The Christs That Rose

In the year 384 A.D. a swarthy and remarkable young man of thiry years entered Rome and gazed for the first time upon its splendors and gaieties. He came from Roman Africa, and he was going to make a fortune by teaching rhetoric in Rome. His name Augustinus; and he little dreamed that until about the year 1950 A.D., or thereabouts, he would be known all over the world, and greatly honored, under the quaint name of St. Augustine.

In *Life and Morals in Greece and Rome** we may see something of the superb city and wonderful life which Augustine would admire. Here I am going to tell one experience which he described in later years. He was not yet a Christian: neither was Rome, for he tells us that even then, three centuries and a half after the death of Christ, seventy years after the Emperors had begun to make an acceptance of Christianity "the pathway of ambition," still "nearly the whole nobility of Rome"—which means the whole of its educated men—were pagans. Imperial gold had built a church or two, but the great city of a million people scorned the new religion. It had a score

---

*Little Blue Book No. 1078

of more attractive religions; and it was the very popular annual procession through the streets of one of these that Augustine saw.

This was in March, 385 A.D., the beginning of spring in Rome, and when the priests of Cybele, "the mother of the gods," celebrated their "holy week." It had begun with a procession, on March 17 when priests and devotees carried reeds: as they carry palms in a Catholic church on the first day of Holy Week in our time. Five days later—Sunday to Friday is five days—there was a second solemn procession. The priests bore a sacred emblem through the streets to the temple on the Palatine Hill; and the emblem was the figure of a beautiful young god, pale in death, bound to a small pine tree, which was crowned with violets. Attis was dead, and the procession went its way with ceremonial sadness.

The next day was the "Day of Blood." Attis had bled, and his priests and worshipers must bleed. In the full ritual of the cult of Attis and Cybele, in the east, the priests tore from their bodies the organs of manhood and held aloft their great sacrifice to the mother and divine lover. Rome did not permit this; but priests and worshipers gashed themselves and made the blood flow; and drums thundered, and howls of lamentation rose, and the enuch priests rent their flowing robes. Attis was dead: the beautiful Attis.

And on the next day he rose from the dead. It was the *Hilaria* ("Day of Hilarity"), a very popular Roman festival, when all things were lawful, because your heart rejoiced to know that Attis had come to life again. Two days later was the part of the festival at which Augustine assisted. The priests took the black stone (phallic stone) with a silver head, which represented Cybele, for a ceremonious bath in the Almo; and they return through Rome, with horns blowing and drums throbbing, frantic with rejoicing, while the two great hedges of Roman spectators supported them with an orgy of sexual songs and jokes and embraces. The spirit of love was born again.

It was long years afterwards, when Augustine had become a very solemn and very sour and very puritanical bishop, that he described these things. I need not reproduce his comments. But he hints that at the time the religious life he saw in Rome made him lean to the Academic philosophy (an early type of Agnosticism). His mother Monica was a Christian, and she sought the conversion of her son with all the fire with which she had once sought a lover. But Augustine smiled disdainfully at the Christian Church in Rome.

Although he does not say so explicitly, one reason for his aversion must have been the sight of these two Holy Weeks. In the same month as the pagans the Christians opened a Holy Week with a plam-bearing procession, and five days later they mourned before the figure of a pale young god nailed to a "tree" (as they chanted), and two days later again they went into a frenzy of rejoicing because he had risen from the dead. The one Holy Week was a frank drama of the death and resurrection of love: the other was, at least in theory, a spiritual and ascetic drama. But Augustine would look from the pale young Attis on his tree to the pale young Christ on his cross, from resurrection to resurrection, and wonder . . . Cybele and Attis were ages older than Jesus.

The modern American Christian who may in some audacious moment open the opulent pages of Sir J. G. Frazer's *Golden Bough* (especially the volume *Adonis, Attis, Osiris*) and read about this ancient cult of a slain and resurrected god, has at first a strange fluttering of the heart; then he sets it all aside with a forced laugh. This, he says, is "science." Guessing again: theories. He sees in the footnotes a formidable list of authorities. They are all Greek and Latin and Arabic and German. He can't read a word of them—not even if the books existed in the United States.

So I introduce the matter on the authority of one before whom the Christians must bow in silence. Augustine saw this in Rome, in the year 385; just before paganism was fiercely persecuted and suppressed by the men who wrote pathetic books about the persecutions they had suffered.

And there was in Rome about the same time another very learned man to whose authority every Christian must bow, St. Jerome. In his *Commentary on Ezekiel* St. Jerome says (I translate the Latin):

> Hence as, according to the pagan legend, the lover of Venus, a most beautiful youth, is said to have been slain, then raised to life again, in the month of June, they call the month of June by his name, and they have a solemn celebration in it every year, in the course of which his death is mourned by the women, and afterwards his resurrection is chanted, and praised. (Migne edition of Jerome's works, vol. XXV, col. 82.)

Jerome, who spent a large part of his life in Palestine, is speaking of the east—the whole region of Palestine and Mesopotamia—and the "most beautiful youth" is Tammuz. The goddess whom he calls "Venus," in Roman fashion, is really the Babylonian Ishtar, the Astarte of the Phoenicians and the Hebrews. Attis, to whom I have referred above, was the slain and resurrected god of the Phrygians: "the Lord," as he was known over all that part of the earth, whether priests called him Tammuz or Attis. "Lord" is in Palestinian language "Adon." Even the Bible sometimes gives Adonai (really Adoni—"my lord") as a name for God; and the Greeks took it for a proper name and created the beautiful young god "Adonis," the lover of Venus, who died and rose again every year.

And they were not surprised, because they thought nothing of bringing the dead to life. Asclepios had brought so many dead back to life that the monarch of the world of the dead got jealous and had him slain; and, being a god, he in a sense rose from the dead. Anyhow, other gods of Greek mythology had died and risen from the dead; and so, when this fascinating ritual of a holy week came along to Greece from Syria, the women quite generally adopted it.

Thus in every land where Christianity spread the slain and resurrected god, and the dramatic annual celebration of his death and resurrection, were quite familiar. It was Tammuz all over the plains of Mesopotamia, from Ur of the Chaldees to Jerusalem. It was Attis all over the region to the north and northwest of Palestine and through the old Phoenician civilization on the coast of Palestine and Asia Minor. It was Adonis in Greece, then in Rome, and gradually all over the Greco-Roman world. We may be sure that Agustine had seen it in Carthage before he went to Rome. We may almost suppose that the Romans took it with them to Spain and Gaul, if not Britain.

I may seem to have overlooked Egypt; but Egypt was precisely the classic home of the myth of a slain and resurrected god. "I am the Resurrection and the Life" is merely an epitome of what the Egyptians chanted for ages about their great god Osiris, the judge of the dead, one of the oldest and most revered gods of Egypt. He had been slain by "the powers of darkness" embodied in his wicked brother, Set. His sister and wife, Isis, had sought the fragments of his body and put them together again. And he had arisen from the dead, and was enthroned in the world of souls, to judge every man according to his works. The resurrection of Osiris was the basis of the Egyptian's firm hope of eternal life. Every year the fair strip of land along the Nile mourned for days over the slaying of Osiris and then rejoiced exceedingly over his resurrection.

You may nervously say, you may hope, that all this is really later than the death and resurrection of Jesus. . . . Queer how my pen stumbles over that word. It wants always to write "Christ"; and the explanation may be interesting, even instructive.

From forty to thirty years ago I was a monk of the

Order of St. Francis, and we were taught never to pronouce the name "Jesus" except in prayer, and to bow our heads whenever it was pronounced. If ever we saw it on a piece of paper that lay about we were reverently to burn the paper. Ten years stamped that so deeply on my nerves that even now, in my learned and blasphemous age, with the entire story of religion through the ages unfolded before my mind, I hesitate a little to use the word Jesus. That is parable. Apply it to religious psychology and the religious instinct and the sentiment of faith. All are the product of education and environment.

You may, then, say impulsively, that somehow the Christian belief in the death and resurrection of Jesus got amongst the pagan religions, and they borrowed it. Many desperate things have been said by religious apologists, but I am not aware that any one of them ever said that. He would have to be very remarkably indifferent to the absurdity of his statements. Augustine and Jerome lived in the fourth century, it is true; but neither they nor any other Christian Fathers dreamed of saying that the pagans had borrowed from Christianity. It took them all their time to defend their own church from the charge of borrowing from the pagans. Every apologist has to meet that scornful charge from Jews and pagans.

However, one must put aside at once any idea of these slain and resurrected gods being modeled on Jesus. It is as absurd as it would be to say that the biography of Julius Caesar was modeled on that of Napoleon!

Cyril (Bishop) of Alexandria refers to the celebration as of very ancient date. It never occurs to him that the pagans borrowed it. He says (*Commentary on Isaiah*, II, 3):

> The Greeks *invented* a solemnity in which they mourned with Venus for the death of Adonis, and then affected to rejoice when they found returning from the underworld him whom they sought; and this ridiculous cere-

mony took place in the temples of Alexandria down
to our own time.

A much earlier Father of the Church was Firmicus Maternus: the most stupid man who ever wrote a valuable book.
The book is called *The Errors of the Profane Religions,*
and it is a treasury of the pagan beliefs and ceremonies
which the Church Christianized. Firmicus cheerfully con-
cluded that the devil had given the world these legends
in advance so as to spoil the chances of Christianity when
it came. So all the early Christians thought. He says (Ch.
II) of the Egyptians:

> They have in a temple an image of Osiris buried, and
> this they honor with an annual lamentation. They shave
> their heads . . . they beat their breasts. And when they
> have done this for a few days, they pretend that they
> have found the fragments of the torn body (of Osiris),
> and they lay aside their grief and rejoice.

So a modern Chinese student might write home to his
wondering mother after seeing the Holy Week ceremonies
in some Catholic church of the United States today! And
notice that Alexandria has two slain and resurrected gods.
Cyril has told us, above, of the worship there of Adonis
or Tammuz. In fact, it had at least three (and most probably
more) annual resurrections, for the worship of the Persian
god Mithra flourished there, as everywhere else; and the
Mithraists, as Firmicus expressly tells us (I will give the
passage later), every year laid a statue of Mithra on a
bier, mourned his death, and then, in a blaze of candles,
rejoiced at his resurrection. And Alexandria did not differ
from the other cosmopolitan cities of the time. It is in
Rome that Firmicus describes the Mithraist celebration—
Augustine, doubtless, saw that also—and of the Adonis
ceremony he says: "In most cities of the east Adonis is
mourned as the husband of Venus and . . . his wound is

exhibited to the spectators." I have to translate these passages from the Latin or Greek for my readers, as religious writers do not seem anxious to put them before their modern followers. I use the famous Migne edition of the Fathers, the work of the learned Benedictine monks—who at one time really were learned, and correspondingly liberal—and I notice that the monastic editors, finding these constant references to the deaths and resurrections of pagan gods, make this comment in a footnote: "This dramatic representation, in which a dead man (god) was mourned and was honored in the dark, with chanted lamentations, until, the lights being lit, the mourning turned to joy, we find in different forms in almost all the mysteries" (vol. XII, col. 1032). Now, those "mysteries," whether Egyptian, Babylonian, Phoenician, Persian, Phrygian, or Greek, go back to long before the time of Christ. Plutarch, in his *Lives* ("Alcibiades," XVIII), speaking of the sailing of the Greek fleet for Syracuse in the year 415 B.C., says: "It was an evil omen that the festival of Adonis fell in those days. Numbers of women bore images, like dead bodies, and held mock funerals; and they mourned and chanted the solemn hymns." He wrote also a whole treatise on the Egyptian cult of Isis and Osiris.

But the Bible itself takes us back to the fifth century. The passage I quoted from Jerome is in a commentary on *Ezekiel,* in which we read (VIII, 14): "And behold there sat women weeping for Tammuz." So several centuries before Christ the lamentations over Tammuz, to be followed by jubilation over his resurrection, had spread from the dying empire of Babylon to Judea.

And there is much earlier reference in the Bible which is rarely noticed. The passage I quoted from Cyril of Alexandria is found in his *Commentary on Isaiah.* The bishop has arrived at this very obscure passage (XVIII, 1-2):

Woe to the land shadowing with wings which is beyond the rivers of Ethiopia:

> That sendeth ambassadors by the sea, even in ves-
> sels of bulrushes upon the waters, saying: Go, ye swift
> messengers, to a nation scattered and peeled, etc.

This is abominably mistranslated from the Hebrew text.
If the reader cares to compare various translations of the
Bible in different languages, he will see that none of the
translators understood the passage. But Cyril of Alexandria did. The Greek text of the prophet which he uses
says plainly, "That sendeth *hostages by the sea and letters
of papyrus* upon the water"—and Cyril tells us what this
means.

As I will show in the fourth chapter, the Egyptians
said in their legend that the body of Osiris floated to
Byblus, on the coast of Syria, and Isis went there to re-
cover it. Cyril gives the whole legend of Adonis—I will
reproduce his words later—and rightly identifies Adonis
with Tammuz and even with Osiris. Then, to explain the
"letters of papyrus" in *Isaiah*, he tells us that every year
the "friends of Venus" (priestesses of Aphrodite) mourned
at Byblus, and the women of the land "beyond the rivers
of Ethiopia," the land (to translate the Hebrew text cor-
rectly) "of the fluttering of the wings of birds," wrote a
letter on papyrus, put it on a raft, and sent it out to sea.
It was supposed to float to Byblus and to inform the
"friends of Venus" that her lover's body had been found,
and so their mourning turned into the joy of the
resurrection.

Sir J. G. Frazer has evidently been himself puzzled
at this point. He overlooks the important passage in *Isaiah*,
and considers that the connection of Osiris with Byblus
(which is given in Plutarch) is a late addition to the legend.
"Byblos" is not only the name of the city of Aphrodite
in Syria, but it is also the Greek word for "papyrus," the
material on which the Egyptians wrote, so Frazer thinks
that some Greek writer got confused between the two.
If he had carefully studied Cyril of Alexandria, he would

have realized how interesting the matter is. Isaiah—the genuine prophet Isaiah, not the forger of the second part—plainly says, about the year 700 B.C., that in his time the women of Egypt—I am confident that he means simply Egypt, and is confused about the geography—sent a letter yearly to the priestesses of Byblus to turn their laments over the death of Adonis into the joy of resurrection. That is full biblical authority for the death and resurrection celebrations of both Osiris and Tammuz seven hundred years before Jesus was born!

But to any properly informed person these biblical references are as superfluous as it would be to quote the authority of President Wilson for the Declaration of Independence in 1776. The legends and the annual celebrations were already hoary with antiquity when Isaiah and the writer of *Ezekiel* referred to them. This we shall see presently. I have given this introduction to the old myths, on the authority of Christian and biblical writers, merely to prepare the reader for a candid examination of the myths of the resurrection which we find in the New Testament.

2

The Gospel Fairy Tale

It is not probable that one modern Christian out of one hundred thousand knows that centuries before the time of Christ the nations annually celebrated the death and resurrection of Osiris, Tammuz, Attis, Mithra, and other gods. Tell it to your neighbor, and he will laugh. That is, he will say, the "science" of comparative religion. But I write these books in the hope that directly or indirectly, they will reach Christians. I am giving a full, serious, simple, and easily verified examination of the Christian creed in every aspect; and this aspect with which I now deal is one of the most important, and to me most fascinating, aspects. So I approach it on lines on which any believer may accompany me.

What will he say? Surely not, as the early Christians did, that the devil inspired the pre-Christian nations with these resurrection myths. That is, frankly, childish. We shall in the end search for, and probably find, the real roots of the myth in the early mind of the race. I take it that my religious reader will be puzzled. He ought to have known these things before. Why cannot his writers and preachers candidly face them? All that I ask him to do for the moment is to make, with me, a more careful examination than he has ever made before of the evidence for the resurrection in the New Testament.

There is a remarkable difference between the evidence for the virgin birth and that for the resurrection. I must here assume that the reader has seen *Did Jesus Ever Live?* (Little Blue Book No. 1084),* in which I discuss the age and respective value, or lack of value, of the various writings of the New Testament. Paul comes first: then *Mark* (except the last part): and so on. Now the earlier parts know nothing whatever about a miraculous birth of Jesus, but they are quite certain of the resurrection. Unless we deny the genuineness of the whole of the Epistles, which is a desperate venture, Paul was absolutely convinced of the resurrection; and this proves that it was widely believed not many years after the death of Jesus. His insistence in the Epistles shows, of course, that it was disputed. The statement was a "piece of folly" and a "stumbling block" to the converts from paganism; precisely because they saw resurrection-celebrations every year. But the belief existed, and Paul was sure of it, within a few years of the crucifixion.

Well, let us examine the story as it is told by the writers of the Gospels. *Mark,* the oldest Gospel, has the simplest account: that is to say, *Mark* as you read it in your American bible today. It is the easiest thing in the world to prove that these Gospels have received additions and interpolations. Turn to *Matthew* xxviii 19: "Go ye, therefore, and teach all nations, baptizing them in the name of the Father, and of the Son, and of the Holy Ghost." Not only had Jesus given his disciples exactly the opposite instructions (*Matthew* x 5-7), but he certainly never baptized, or ordered the baptism of, anybody; and he never taught any cut-and-dried Trinitarian doctrine of Father, Son and Holy Ghost. It took the Church three centuries to settle these matters. Even orthodox theologians, in fact,

---

*In this volume. (Ed.)

admit that this ending has been flagrantly tacked on to the Gospel of *Matthew* in the fourth century.

Now the oldest manuscripts of *Mark* end at v 8 of ch. xvi. The rest of the last chapter is in an entirely different style, and it flatly contradicts what precedes. In v 7 an angel says to the women: "Go your way, tell his disciples and Peter that he goeth before you into Galilee; there shall ye see him, as he said unto you." According to the writer of the Gospel as it originally was, the three women told nobody, for they were afraid. So the new writer (v 9) makes jesus appear in person to one of the women, and she goes to tell the "mourning and weeping" disciples. They refuse to believe; and a second apparition was heard of by them with the same refusal to believe. These clever men had, presumably, seen daily proof for two or three years that Jesus was God, and *Mark* says that he had foretold his resurrection to them; but they stubbornly refused to believe in his power to come to life again and they timorously thought that the whole business was ended! The entire passage from v 9 onward is preposterous.

But the earlier part is not much better. The three women went early on a Sunday morning to "anoint" the body of (God) with "spices." How you anoint a body with spices I do not know; or why they waited until two days after the burial. In Judea in April no one would dream of anointing a body two days dead; and Jewish laws permitted them to go after sunset on Saturday. Moreover, they are supposed to know that the tomb is closed with a stone which they cannot move, but they take no man with them, and they idly wonder (v 3) how they can get it done. Then they find "a young man" sitting inside (what one sits on in a tomb is not clear); and, of course, they cannot tell an angel when they see one—and even the word of an angel only frightens them; and we are asked to believe that three gossipy Jewish women—it would be a greater miracle than the resurrection—had these tremendous experiences, and were expressly ordered to tell them, yet went home and told nobody, even that the body of the Lord was missing!

The truth is that the whole final narrative of *Mark* is a tissue of interpolations and contradictions. Joseph of Arimathea had already (xv 46) had the body properly prepared for burial. Even the officer in charge of the soldiers is made to say, at the cross: "Truly this man was the Son of God." A likely expression for a Roman officer; but the chief point is that with all these portents all the relatives and followers of Jesus are smitten with grief and confusion. They are supposed to know that the most sublime thing in history has happened under their eyes: God in human shape has died and released mankind from the curse. Yet they weep copiously, and are "amazed," "afraid," and slink off into quiet corners to whisper to each other. It is a most clumsy fabrication. Obviously, some early life of Jesus, in which he was conceived merely as a good man, and was correspondingly mourned, has been crudely tampered with by these later resurrection- ists; and, as the first interpolations were not strong enough, more were added. The Church, which the Catholic imag- ines as "guarding the deposit of revelation" was improving it every half century.

Matthew has another, and still later version, complete- ly contradicting *Mark*. The tomb is here supposed to be sealed by the Jewish authorities, and a guard set over it. That is to say, the most learned of the Jews are supposed to think that Jesus had foretold his resurrection—while the disciples are uniformly represented as refusing to believe it when it did occur—and thinking that there might be a melodramatic attempt to steal the body and say that he was risen. Then there is a "great earthquake" (not other- wise recorded), and even this is not enough to shift the stone, so an "angel of the Lord" (a pure spirit) comes down and puts his shoulder to it, and then sits on it (outside the tomb, not *inside*, as *Mark* says), presumably wiping his brow. And the angel's countenance is "like lightning," etc. Yet the ladies in *Mark* merely thought him a strange "young man," and took no notice of his orders; while *Matthew* makes them see a squad of hardy soldiers tremble before his glory.

In *Matthew,* moreover, the two women (who are three in *Mark*), instead of getting a fright and remaining miraculously dumb, run at once, with "great joy" to tell the disciples. Another touch is added by making Jesus appear to them on the way to Jerusalem; whereas *Mark* makes the first apparition to one woman only, and at a later date. Then these chocolate soldiers are supposed to go and tell the high priests about the strange business, and the priests bribe them to say that they all fell asleep on sentry duty. In Ch. xxvii (v 65) Pilate has refused a squad of Roman soldiers, and has told the priests to use their own police, which they did. In Ch. xxviii (v 14) the police have turned into Roman soldiers, responsible to "the Governor" (who has expressly refused to have anything to do with the matter); but they are quite willing, for a few dollars, to expose themselves to sentence of death (for sleeping on sentry duty—no priest could save a Roman soldier from sentence for *that*). But, of course, this is only "*if* it comes to the governor's ears" (v 14); and a trifle such as a resurrection from the dead, in a quiet city like Jerusalem, was not likely to reach his ears.

Then the disciples are told to go to a secret rendezvous on a mountain in Galilee if they wish to see the risen Lord. They do not believe a word of it, but they go, and they see him. A human body transfigured (now that it no longer lives an earthly life) by an indwelling divine spirit ought to be a wonderful spectacle. No: "some of them doubted." It must have been a very ordinary sight . . . I really cannot go on. It is too childish for words. Let us try *Luke*.

Luke (being a doctor, they say) provides the women— there are now "certain others with them"—with "oint-

ments" as well as spices; though he has already made
Joseph of Arimathaea have the body properly prepared
and interred. They do not see a shining angel sitting on
the stone outside, smiling at a squad of terror-stricken
soldiers (or policemen), as *Matthew* says, or "a young
man" sitting inside, as *Mark* says. But "two men in shining
garments" (strange how persistently Jewish women can't
recognize angels) suddenly appear and tell them. They
run home and remind the disciples that Jesus had really
foretold that he would rise on the third day; a detail which
everybody had forgotten. The disciples call this an "idle
tale." They think, apparently, according to all the Gospels,
that the Jesus they knew was not in the least likely to
rise from the dead. It is a nightmare of mysteries—or contradictory inventions.

Then a new version is drawn upon. Some Christian
group which follows Peter in opposition to Paul makes
him "run" to the tomb; though in the preceding verse he
has pooh-poohed the "idle tale." He finds the shroud; and,
unfortunately, he does not tell us what Jesus wore when
he left this behind. Peter was alone; but the John group
in the Church wouldn't have this, so in *John* (xx 3) Peter
runs a race up the hill with John, and is beaten. In *John*
also the details about the linen multiply; naturally, as it
is an older Gospel, and the peculiar character of the Gospel narratives is that the farther a writer is removed from
the events, the more he knows. Paul knows very little:
Mark a little more than Paul: *Matthew* and *Luke* (about
the end of the century) still more: and *John* (well in the
second century) knows everything.

However, *Luke*, "the physician," makes Jesus, who
now has no metabolism in his transfigured body, walk
a few miles with two of the dicsiples; and so naturally
that they never for a moment suspected his identity,
though he proved at great length to them how Jesus was
bound to die and rise again. He seems to have trodden
the dust of the road with them for several hours. However,

they go home in great excitement, when they at last realize that their casual acquaintance on the road is God, and they tell the others. And Jesus, who in the two earlier Gospels refuses to meet the disciples in Jersualem, and appoints a melodramatic meeting-place in Galilee, now appears to them in the city. Although they had been so well prepared (as well as by three years of miracles) they were "terrified and affrighted." Even the marks of the nails on his hands and feet left them skeptical. The only thing that could convince them was, curiously enough, to see that he could eat fish and honey. Finally, in flat contradiction to the earlier Gospels, Jesus tells them not to leave Jerusalem, and they boldly invade the temple and sing the whole story at the top of their voices.

After this we need not linger over *John.* Another decade or two have added materially to the legend. Now we learn that Nicodemus and Joseph *did* anoint the body of Jesus; and very effectively, because they are said to have used about a hundredweight of myrrh and aloes (xix 39–40). So Mary Magdalene does not take spices. She is alone, moreover, and she sees no angel and no policemen. She runs home and tells Peter (and, of course, John), and they run a race; and they see no angels; and we are still told, for some mysterious reason, that they had no recollection whatever of Jesus saying that he would rise again. However, Mary goes back—still alone—and sees two angels; and even in face of this glorious vision she sobs and complains that somebody has stolen the body of Jesus. One would think that there were body-snatchers in ancient Judea.

We will suppose that the bright eyes of the retired sinner were dimmed with tears, for the next verse is too strong, even for Orientals: Jesus, the transfigured godman, appears to her, and she thinks that he is the gardener and that he stole the body! "Woman," he says harshly to his friend; but the next moment he whispers tenderly "Mary," and her eyes are opened. "Rabboni" ("My Rabbi"—

just what Jesus had said nobody ought to be called), she cries, and apparently . . . anyhow, he has to say, "touch me not." So she tells the disciples, and *John* agrees with *Luke* against *Mark* and *Matthew*, that Jesus *did* appear to the disciples in jerusalem, and that the melodramatic rendezvous on a mountain in Galilee is piffle.

In fact, Jesus appeared *twice* to them, *John* says; and, although he walked through a locked door, one of them, "doubting Thomas," wouldn't believe that he was God until he saw that there was a wound in his side. *John* does, it is true, then send them to Galilee. But it is funny. After Jesus has breathed the Holy Ghost on to them (xx 22), and given them such terrific powers as that of absolving from sin, they return to their humble profession of fishermen on the Sea of Tiberias! And they have to be convinced all over again—by the usual strange evidence of eating—and then, appearently, they go back to business once more.

My dear Christian friend, do you really expect me to take all this seriously? I am accustomed to a critical study of historical documents, and this . . . It is the most appalling jumble of contradictions, and the tale grows under our eyes in the course of the first century. It is as crude as anything in ancient mythology. There is not the slightest pretense of consistency in the various versions and successive additions to the original story. Let us turn to *Paul*, and see if we can ascertain what the original story was.

We get little help from *Acts*. The author repeats what he has said in *Luke* about apparitions, and he enlarges a little upon the ascension; which is not known to any other writer. Jesus, we are asked to believe, took his disciples (as usual) up a "mountain," and from there he rose physically in the air until he disappeared in a cloud. It is perfectly amazing to find people in the twentieth century who regard such statements as historical. It is just the myth of Hercules ascending to heaven in a cloud.

Paul's Epistles are the earliest documents; and they give us to understand that the followers of Jesus believed in his resurrection and his appearances to various friends at least a few years after his death. On any serious canon of evidence that is the only witness to the resurrection that we can be asked to consider. The Gospel stories are late, contradictory, and often absurd. Paul's Epistles were, of course, written long after the death of Jesus, but we must clearly put back his belief in the Resurrection to the time of his conversion. He was convinced by the followers of Jesus at Jerusalem that the prophet had risen from the dead and had been seen by Peter and by the whole eleven (somewhere he says twelve) apostles.

There are certain details in Paul which must be considered. The Epistles are very sparing in details—these had not yet been invented—but *Acts* puts into the mouth of Paul a speech made in the synagogue at Antioch. In this speech Paul plainly says that it was, as we should normally expect, the Jewish authorities who buried Jesus; and in that case his body would be put in the common pit for the burial of crucified criminals. Paul says (*Acts* xiii 27–29):

> For they that dwell at Jerusalem, and their rulers, because they knew him not, nor yet the voices of the prophets which were read every Sabbath day, they have fulfilled them in condemning him . . .
> And when they had fulfilled all that was written of him, they took him down from the tree, and laid him in a sepulcher.

This flatly denies all the picturesque details in the Gospels. If a companion of Paul wrote this, as all suppose, the first story of the resurrection was quite different from that in the Gospels. Paul was a Jew, and he knew Jewish law; which not a single Gospel writer seems to have done. There was no need whatever to wait until Sunday morning. The Sabbath prohibition of work ended at sunset. The whole Gospel story is a fiction that could only grow and find acceptance amongst foreigners.

Paul, on the other hand, is the only writer who makes Jesus appear to five hundred at a time. It is amusing to find Christian writers emphasizing this "large number" of witnesses to the resurrection. *We have not a single witness to the resurrection.* None of the women or men who are supposed to have gone to the tomb and seen Jesus has left us any testimony. A late writer forged a Gospel in the name of John. A still later writer forged in the name of Peter a Gospel with such fantastic details about the resurrection that even the early Christians, whose faith was great, rejected it. And evidently this story of an apparition to five hundred, which circulated early, was in the course of time considered too strong, and was abandoned.

In the end, therefore, we come down to the single statement of Paul that the Jewish authorities cast the body of Jesus into the pit, but some of his followers said that Jesus subsequently appeared to them, and so he must have risen from the dead. Some believed this, and others disbelieved. Paul's insistence implies that, and in one place (*I Cor.* xv 12) he says that some Christians do not believe in the resurrection of the dead. It was, however, generally believed, and it is useless now to ask how the belief arose. Clearly, according to the earliest versions, the apostles scattered when Jesus was arrested, and they returned to their work as fishermen. Later they said that they had "seen the Lord"—such details as those about the women are far later in appearance—and they resumed preaching in his name. Is it a novel thing in religious history for enthusiasts to see visions? Quite the contrary. Down to our own time, in Spiritualism, it is the most common of experiences. Scores of Roman Catholic saints claim to have seen Jesus in the flesh; and the Portestant denies every word of it.

The belief in the resurrection is thus a quite normal event; especially as Jesus was held to be the Messiah, and the resurrection of the Messiah was held to have been predicted. But the elaborate story in the Gospels is not merely a myth. It is a fairy tale; and we clearly see the growth of it from 50 A.D. to 120 A.D. Whether or not the world-wide belief in the resurrection of gods disposed the followers of Jesus to believe in his resurrection, the growth of the story, as the decades went on, is plainly influenced by the other myths, and we will consider them more closely.

3

The Mourning over Tammuz

There seems to be no doubt whatever amongst biblical scholars, critical or orthodox, that Isaiah wrote the passage I have quoted in the last chapter. It must therefore have been written before the year 700 B.C. The Egyptian alliance was then a burning question in Judea. But the Hebrews had very dim ideas about geography, and Isaiah apostrophizes the land "beyond the rivers of Ethiopia," the land "of the rustling of the wings of birds." He plainly means Egypt, and it is natural to assume that he refers to the Delta region, where flocks of birds lived amongst the reeds. He does not say, as Frazer does, that they floated letters on the river but on the sea.

From here, he says, the women send letters on rafts to some people abroad, and Cyril, living on the coast of Egypt, gives us the meaning. Every year the Egyptian devotees of Osiris and Isis float a message in the sea to the devotees or priestesses of Astarte at Byblus. Neither the Roman Venus nor the Greek Aphrodite was known in the east in those days. The goddess whose "friends" mourned in Byblus was the Phoenician Astarte, a variant of the Babylonian ishtar. The divine lover whose death the priestesses mourned was the Phoenician Adonis, "the

Lord" (*Adon*) Tammuz of Babylonia. We shall see in the next chapter what the Egyptians and their god Osiris had to do with Byblus. For the moment we will inquire what Byblus was, and what happened there.

Byblus, which claimed to be the oldest city of the Phoenicians, was famous at least in the millennium before Christ, for its magnificent temple of Astarte. It was on a height, not far from the sea, and travelers still find there a massive piece of masonry which seems to have been the pedestal of a column. We know, in fact, that the chief object of veneration, the emblem of the goddess, in the great open court of the temple, was a phallic stone: a tall cone or obelisk. Astarte was, very frankly, the goddess of love, and her sanctuary was an unblushing garden of love. But with Astarte was associated a handsome young male god, Adonis ("the Lord"). How could people be satisfied with a goddess of love without a lover? At all events, where, as we have repeatedly seen, two deities had to be accommodated in the religion of a people, or the claims of two rival priesthoods adjusted, they were mated as brothers, or husband and wife, or mother and son, and so on. This was generally effected by a priest-made legend. We see in the volume on Egypt* that there were in that country three of four colleges of priests which were centers for the manufacture of legends; and we learn in the volume on the Old Testament† that the priestly college of the Jews was equally enterprising.

In the older nations, which did not take these legends with all the fierce solemnity with which the Jews held theirs, the stories were modified and enlarged as time went on, and I will give the legend of Astarte and Adoni in its last form, as Lucian, Plutarch, and Cyril give it, just before the sun of Syria was darkened by the shadow of the cross, and the scent of the myrtles and cooing of the

---

*Little Blue Book No. 1977
†Little Blue Book No. 1066

doves of Astarte were thrust into the horrid category of sins.

King Cinyras, says Cyril with great scorn, was fabled by the Phoenicians to have yielded to a passion for his beautiful daughter Myrrha at a harvest festival, and to have engendered the lovely child Adoni. We are by this time familiar with the naiveté of the pagan world. Their families of gods mingled incessantly with mortals. There was no abyss of stupendous awe and majesty between mortals and immortals. A goddess espied a handsome youth in the river and came down to him; or Zeus, perhaps, caught sight of a maiden in her bath. These pagans, we must remember, still lay in darkness and the shadow of death. One must not expect them to rise to the height of a god who passes sentence of damnation on the whole race for one woman's peccadillo, or burns a maid for all eternity for listening to the whisper of the heart he has created in her.

Well, to return to Cyril and the legend. The king was ashamed—it is more probable that here we have another variant of the monarch who seeks the life of the new-born divine child—and he had the infant cast away on a mountain. But the nymphs or spirits of the mountain adopted it, and the child grew to be a male beauty and a great hunter; and one day, as he hunted, Astarte saw and fell in love with him. In another and probably older version, Astarte was also his mother, having fallen in love with the handsome Cinyras.

In fact, there is a whole thicket of interesting myths here. Cinyras was a real name of Phoenician kings of the island of Cyprus, and this legendary Cinyras was the son of the legendary king Pygmalion, who fell in love with a statue of Astarte (or Aphrodite) and took it to bed. (It is the later Roman poet Ovid who makes Pygmalion a sculptor who falls in love with a statue.) Pygmalion, Cinyras, and Adoni were all said to be very handsome and amorous, and to have instituted sacred prostitution in the temples of Astarte and lit the flame of sensuality over the entire region.

But let us return to St. Cyril. You will prefer his chaster language to my somewhat free discourse. He says:

> They say that Venus, the brazen hussy, saw him there (Adoni hunting) and fell in love with him, and copulated with him and embraced him unceasingly. This offended Mars, the rival for the affections of Venus, and he assumed the form of a wild boar and killed Adoni while he was hunting. Whereat Venus mourned exceedingly. She was so overcome with grief and fear that she went down into the lower regions to bring back her lover. But Pluto's wife saw the beauty of the youth, and she would not let him go; and they came to an agreement that they would divide the year into halves, and each in turn should have him for a season. When Venus announced this to her friends and worshippers, the event was made a feast or celebration.

Cyril then writes the passages which I quoted in the first chapter: that the Greeks invented a death and resurrection festival, and that the women of Egypt united with the women of Phoenicia by sending a letter on the waves. As Isaiah tells us, all this was done ages before anybody in the east ever heard of "Greeks"; but, of course, a learned Father of the Church cannot be expected to have the foggiest notion of history or geography. We can be sure that at least in the second millennium before Christ the Phoenicians of the north and the islands annually celebrated the death of Adoni, the mourning of Astarte, and the glorious reunion of the ethereal lovers. We will go beyond that presently.

Sir J. G. Frazer dwells with particular elegance and affection on this exotic section of his survey of religion, and I advise the reader to enjoy at least his volume *Adonis, Attis, Osiris.* He describes a beautiful valley some distance east of Byblus, which was known in antiquity as the Vale of Adonis. Here Astarte met the youth, or here she wept over his torn body—the legends differ—and the river Adonis still runs red with the blood of the god once a year (though modern chemists put a more prosy interpretation on the redness), and the red anemones glow in the woods, and the maids of Syria used to mourn, as Mary mourned at the tomb; but only for a season, as Adoni was to rise again from the lower regions ("he descended into hell." Professor Osborn and Professor Pupin solemnly recite in their creed today), and love would again refresh and adorn this weary world.

The Phoenicians very early extended their rule and civilization to the rich island of Cyprus, a day's sail away across the Mediterranean, and here was the second great center of the cult of Astarte and Adoni and love. It is possible that much of the learned work of Frazer and others in this field will have to be reconsidered. When they began, our knowledge of ancient history was wrong. We knew Phoenicia, as the great naval power, and Egypt and Babylonia and Greece. We had some knowledge, too, of a powerful kingdom of a mysterious people called the Hittites, to the north of Palestine. But we did not know that there was as great a civilization as any of them in the island of Crete, and that its fleet mastered the sea, and kept the Phoenicians in the position of small pirates until about 1500 B.C. I will return to this later.

Probably after the fall of Crete the Phoenicians took over Cyprus, and it was there that they located the amorous adventures of Pygmalion and Cinyras. On the southwestern side of the island, about a mile from the blue sea, is the miserable modern village of Kuklia. I know well such places in the neighboring island of Crete, and can picture it. There are Adonises there today by the score: young men of almost feminine loveliness and entirely Phoenician ignorance. Once every year still, as I tell in another volume (*Phallic Elements in Religion*, Little Blue Book No. 1079), the men and women of Kuklia and the district meet at some old stone, and anoint them, and make magico-religious passes and naughty jokes, and believe that this promotes the fertility of their wives. For those stones are the sad relic of the once glorious temple of Astarte and Adoni. This is ancient Paphos, the perfumed garden of love planted amidst the blue waters of the Mediterranean.

On this hill, in the first (and probably second) millennium before Christ stood the beautiful and wicked temple of Aphrodite (or Astarte), where the symbolic doves (now a symbol of innocence!) cooed amorously amongst the pillars, and the pairs of horns (which link the place closely with the ancient Cretans) stood out on the facade, and a great white cone or obelisk in the courtyard unblushingly announced to the world what kind of offering the goddess asked. It was a replica of Byblus: sacred prostitution, and an annual celebration of the death, descent into hell, and return to light of Adoni.

Already before the time of Jesus many religions mingled here. In Cretan ruins three thousand five hundred years old we find the cross, Greek fashion, as perfect as it is in Athenian churches today. In the temple of Paphos were the pairs of horns as in Crete and the star and crescent as in modern Mohammedan Turkey. Greek influence had set in, too, and turned Astarte into Aphrodite, or even Venus. But back of it all is an old, old cult of a great mother goddess, mother earth, the spirit of love and giver of fertility. She was the one deity of the Cretans; though just toward the end of Cretan history we find creeping in the figure of a young god—the strong young god who is to fertilize the divine mother. She was (with a sky-god) a great deity of the Hittites; and Frazer shows that they too had the divine son. She was the Frigga of the Teutons, the Venus of the Romans, the Aphrodite of the Greeks, the Isis of the Egyptians, the Astarte of the Phoenicians and Hebrews, and the Ishtar of the Babylonians.

So we go back a step further in history. Astarte is

the many-thousand-year-old goddess of the Babylonias, Ishtar. Adoni is the equally old, or maybe older, god of Mesopotamia, Tammuz, over whom "the women mourned." He goes back to the days of the old Sumerians, the semi-Mongolian founders of Mesopotamian civilization; and I should not be surprised if, through them, we can one day connect Ishtar with the Shin-Shin-Mo ("Holy Mother") of the Chinese.

At what period in Babylonia history Ishtar was mated with the old god Tammuz, and he was turned into a handsome young lover, we do not know; but the Phoenician version of the myth must itself go back to at least 1500 B.C. I need not give the final legend at length. It is much the same as the Phoenician. Tammuz dies and descends into hell (the lower world), and Ishtar braves all its terrors in search of him. In the little volume on Babylon* I quote an ancient hymn to Ishtar, recounting her devoted search in the home of the dead. While Ishtar was below, the streams of fertility on earth dried up. Nature languished, and love was impotent. The great gods heard the petition of mortals, and the queen of the lower world was forced to compromise. Ishtar was sprinkled with holy water (the Water of Life) and allowed to depart with Tammuz. So every year from the Persian Gulf to the Mediterranean, maids and matrons laid the pale and handsome Tammuz on a bier and mourned; and then the glad tidings of the resurrection spread and an easter joy succeeded the lamentations. The effigy or statue laid on the bier figured a comely young god clad in a red robe; and it was anointed and bathed by the women, who chanted their dirges to the shrill music of flutes, let their long black hair trail in the wind, beat their white breasts, and burned incense to the god.

So popular was the annual celebration with women that even after the stern "reform" of the Jewish religion

---

*Little Blue Book No. 1976

the writer of *Ezekiel*, to his intense disgust, finds the matrons of Jerusalem, with disheveled hair, beating their breasts over the figure of Tammuz within a stone's throw of the temple. Far away in Athens, about the same time, women are making little "gardens of Adonis," flowers and plants set round a bier, and weeping shrilly over the Babylonian god whom their Aphrodite loved. Far to the south, in Alexandria, women, not content with their Osiris, placed little statues of Aphrodite and Adoni on couches, and arranged fruit and flowers and cakes round them, and mourned. In Babylonia itself the festival was in the month of Tammuz (June–July), and the Greeks seem to have adopted the same season, though some writers put it in the spring. At Byblus the solemn celebration was in the spring.

The day of mourning over Tammuz in Babylonia, the seventeenth day of the month Tammuz, was also a kind of All Souls' Day. People made it the occasion of a general commemoration of the spirits or memories of their dead relatives. It is still a fast in the Jewish calendar, showing how thoroughly the cult was once established in Judea; though, of course, the modern Jew thinks that in his fast he is mourning the capture of Jerusalem by the Romans— which took place ages after the fast began. The Christian smiles; but his Good Friday and Resurrection morn are the continuation, under the arc lamps of modern science, of the death and resurrection festivals of the oldest pagan days, and I am not sure that what he calls the sublime theme of his sacred drama—the blood-atonement—is really more elevated than theirs. We will consider that later, and I will close with another quotation from St. Jerome which ought to be equally unpalatable to Jew and Christian. In his *Letter to Paulinus* (Vol. XXII, col. 581, of Migne edition of his works), written from Palestine, he says:

> This Bethlehem which is now ours, and is the most
> august spot on earth, was foreshadowed by a grove

of Tammuz—that is to say, Adonis—in the cave where the infant Christ once wailed the lover of Venus had been mourned.

The man who can think it a coincidence that the birth of Christ was located in a cave in which the rebirth of Tammuz had been celebrated for ages is indeed a man of great faith.

4

The Resurrection of Osiris

So, ages before Christ, a death and resurrection festival was celebrated at Babylon (and further east), Alexandria, and Athens, and in every city that lay between them. Now if you will take the map of the world, and draw a ring with your finger round those three cities, you will find that the circle embraces nearly the whole civilized world of the time. Outside it there remain only Egypt, to the south, and the civilized part of Asia Minor. We shall now see that these regions were as familiar with the death and resurrection celebration as all the other regions of the civilized world.

I began the first chapter with an account of such a celebration in Rome in the year 385 A.D.; and we have historical information that the cult was introduced into Rome in 207 B.C. It was the cult of Attis and Cybele (commonly known as "the mother of the gods"), and it was introduced from Phrygia, in Asia Minor.

North of Phoenicia or Palestine in ancient times was the somewhat obscure kingdom of the Hittites, who were at one time powerful enough to take Babylon. We have found a Hittite monument with three figures which seem to be a trinity of the sky-father, the earth-mother, and a divine son; so it is fair to assume that a more or less similar celebration flourished amongst the Hittites. However that may be, the Phrygians, who covered the region from the west of the Hittite kingdom to the Dardanelles, had one of the most noted cults of a slain and resurrected god.

The great deity of the Phrygians was a nameless "mother of the gods," plainly the old mother-earth goddess. It was a common trick of the priests who rose to power later to give the older gods the title of mother or father of the gods, and, so to say, pension them off. Cybele, as the Greeks named this goddess, remained the supreme deity, as in Crete; but a young male god was closely associated with her. Attis, as he was called, was said in the legend to have been originally a comely young shepherd who was loved by Cybele. He was said to have been born of a virgin. There were two versions of his death. In one he was, like Adoni, slain by a boar: in the other he castrated himself, and bled to death, under a pine tree. The latter is clearly the older legend, a natural incident in a phallic religion; and hence it was that on the great festival the priests of Cybele castrated themselves and held up the bloody organs to the heavens.

I described the modified version of the celebration which was permitted in Rome. March 17th was the day of the reed-bearing procession (Palm Sunday), March 24th was the terrible Day of Blood ("Good" Friday), when the combined din of flutes, horns, cymbals, and tambourines, and the dirges of the processionists, stirred priests and devotees to make their awful sacrifice. The statue of Attis, bound to a pine tree, was carried in procession, and then laid in a temporary sepulcher in the temple; just as the sacrament is, for exactly the same period, put away in a temporary recess or tomb in Roman Catholic churches in Holy Week today. Next day (or two days later) the tomb was opened, and the statue of Attis exhibited amidst frenzied rejoicing. Attis had risen from the dead.

Here is another most dramatic and popular annual celebration of the death and resurrection of a fair young god spreading over the world from an ancient center. Take a citizen, say, of Tarsus in Asia Minor in the days of Jesus. He could not fail to know of the annual celebration of the resurrection of Attis, which was famous all over the Greco-Roman world. He could hardly be ignorant of the festival of the resurrection of Adoni at Byblus and Paphos, both within a short distance of his city. If he were of an inquiring mind, he would know that Adoni was only the Lord Tammuz of the great kindom of Babylonia; and if he were a Jew, he would know that the Jews themselves long mourned the death and rejoiced in the resurrection of Tammuz. Paul was a Jew of Tarsus, of an inquiring mind.

And he would, presumably, know that the Adoni-worshipers of Byblus had a close connection with Egypt, to which we now turn. Many a writer of the time confuses or fuses, as even Cyril of Alexandria does, the cults of Attis, Adonis, Tammuz, and Osiris. A god had been slain and had risen from the dead; and these were merely different names given to the god in different regions. They were wrong. It is a most important feature of our story that this legend of a slain and resurrected god arose in quite different parts of the old civilized world. Tammuz, Attis, and Osiris are three separate and independent creations of the myth-making imagination.

Yet the rites of the mourning over Osiris were much the same as in the case of Adoni. I give in another book the outline of the legend of Isis, Osiris, and Horus but it may be useful to give here a more detailed account of it. The time came in the evolution of religion, as I explained, when the claims of Osiris, Horus, and Isis to the homage of men had to be adjusted. They were made co-equals in a holy family, and gods whose priests were no longer powerful enough to exact, so to say, a place in the front window, were awarded the lesser honor of having given birth to Osiris and Isis, or of being less distinguished or even disreputable members of the same family.

For some reason the old Egyptian god Set was to be discredited, and he was made the murderer of the very popular Osiris: the god who held in Egypt almost the place that Christ had in Christendom. The philosopher Plutarch wrote in the first century a treatise *On Isis and Osiris,* and he gives us the final version of the legend which was current in Egypt. Incidentally he gives us information about the cult of Isis which confirms what I say in another book about, not merely the virtues, but the asceticism, of the later Egyptians. The priests of Isis shaved their heads (and bodies) and wore white linen garments in token of the purity which the religion of Isis demanded. They never ate flesh meat or vegetables that had been in contact with manure; and no wine was admitted into their houses. Salt even was eschewed, since it led to an increase of the appetite for food and drink. In fine, the cult of purity was pushed so far in later Egypt that Plutarch tells us (and seems to believe) that the semen of kings was received in glass tubes and thus conveyed to its destination without the contamination of flesh.

But I am concerned only with the story of Isis and Osiris, and I must greatly abridge the long and rambling story. Nut, the sky-goddess, was the spouse of Ra, the sun-god, who begot Osiris. By a frivolous adventure with Thoth (the divine messenger) she gave birth to Isis, and by a farther intrigue with Seb, the earth-god, to Set. Isis and Osiris so instinctively loved each other that they had relations with each other—unwittingly, Plutarch later says, in the obscurity of the divine mother's womb. Osiris became ruler of Egypt, which he civilized, and he then set out to civilize the world, while Isis cultivated her virginity at home. Both these circumstances enkindled the anger of the saturnine Set (his father, Seb, is the equivalent of the Roman Saturn), the prince of darkness; as Osiris was the prince of light, virtue, and wisdom. He enticed

Osiris to enter a handsome chest, fastened it down with molten lead, and had it flung into the river.

The desolated Isis sought the body of her brother and lover high and low. This search for the missing god or goddess is a common feature, and was dramatically represented in all the old "mysteries." In time she learned that the chest or coffin had been borne by the Nile out to sea, and had been stranded on the coast of Syria near Byblus. Here it became entangled in a tree, which grew to such princely proportions that the king had it cut down and converted (with the coffin inside the trunk) into a column of his palace. Thither came Isis in mortal guise. She accepted the office of nurse to the queen's child, and at night she took the form of a swallow and circled round and round the column. But as she was burning away the mortal flesh of the child, she was recognized, and she departed for Egypt with the column as a gift. Hence the connection of Byblus with Egypt to which I have referred.

Here the legends get even more mixed than the Gospel legends. One story, only briefly referred to by Plutarch, is that in the form of a hawk Isis lay upon the dead body of Osiris and thus miraculously conceived her son Horus. The other legend, which Plutarch follows, is that she left the coffin at a place in Egypt while she went to see Horus. Set found the coffin, cut the corpse into fourteen pieces, and scatted them. Isis made diligent search and found all the pieces but the penis, which the fishes had swallowed. (Frazer here suggests that the legend may recall a prehistoric custom of cutting off a dead king's organ and using it to promote fertility.) However, Isis, to confuse Set, had each of the parts buried where she found it; so that there were fourteen graves of Osiris (besides relics, duplicated and triplicated, in the temples) in Egypt. But Egyptian documents give a finish to the legend which is lacking in Plutarch. Isis and Horus put together the fragments of the dead god, and as the sacred wings of Isis fluttered over the corpse, the great god Ra restored him to life. He "descended into hell" or was appointed the Lord of the Underworld. And it was a common practice after death for an Egyptian priest to mimic this restoration of Osiris over the corpse as a pledge of a glorious resurrection in the kingdom of Osiris.

I can imagine a preacher reading these infantile details and sking what earthly relation there is between this farrago of nonsense and "the sublime story of the resurrection of Jesus." But I explain in the book on *Religion and Morals in Ancient Egypt* (Little Blue Book No. 1077) that Osiris, the Judge of the Dead, was as stern a moral judge as Jesus himself; and, to every Egyptian, personal immortality, prefigured by the resurrection of Osiris, was the firmest of beliefs. The main point is, however, that, when we strip away late embroideries, we have here a doctrine of a beneficent god slain by the powers of darkness and rising again from the dead. The Pyramid Texts—inscriptions on the inner walls of the oldest pyramid tombs—show that this was common Egyptian doctine three thousand years before Christ; and it must go back before the dawn of civilization.

This legend was not only familiar to every child of Egypt as one of the most sacred of his beliefs, but it was annually embodied in a sacred drama or pageant of great solemnity. In the month of November, the period of sowing the corn in Egypt, a famous celebration took place at Sais, one of the centers of the Osiris cult. There were four days of mourning and lamentation over the dead god, whose sufferings were dramatically represented on a lake—I presume, on an island in a lake—at night, while the people illuminated their houses. Three days later the priests bore to the river a golden casket into which they poured water; and at that moment the worshipers raised the cry that Osiris had been found. A gold figure of a cow with a black pall represented Isis during the sacred drama; and the shaven priests and the worshipers beat their breasts and lashed their shoulders. Some even ripped the bandages from healing wounds and let the blood flow. In other places where the passion-play was given, a boy impersonated Osiris, and was "found" by the priests.

Frazer identifies this with the general festival of Osiris which he next described, but it seems to me that the above is a description of the "mysteries" of Osiris to which Plutarch refers. The national festival of Osiris lasted no less than eighteen days and included a most elaborate ritual in the temple. Inscriptions and bas-reliefs in the temples show that the image of Osiris was buried, and in the end he was shown rising from his bier under the spreading wings of Isis. A great feature of the festival, all over Egypt, was the making of images of Osiris with grains of corn planted inside them and gradually growing out of them: a symbol of new life, of the resurrection of the corn-spirit from what was left of the dead plant. Whatever the meaning—we will discuss this later—all Egypt was from time immemorial familiar with a story of a suffering, slain, and risen god, the greatest benefactor of mankind; and, in spite of the phallic elements in the legend, the "easter" of the Egyptians came to be regarded as a time of intense fervor for purity and repentance.

But we have not yet finished with the older pagan world, if we would understand how thoroughly every part of it was saturated with the myth of a resurrected god. We have up to the present said nothing about Persia: the land which took over the supremacy of the world when Babylon, Assyria, and Egypt fell, the religion which spread over the world, from Persepolis to Britain, at the very time when Christianity was a pale growth struggling for existence in that tropical forest of religions.

Mithraism preceded Christianity with an austere belief in a savior from sin who was born of a virgin, in a cave in midwinter, and was annually represented as such before the worshipers in its ascetic temples. And Mithraism also preceded Christianity, by centuries, with an annual representation of the atoning death of Mithra and the joy of his resurrection. It is Firmicus Maternus, the Christian Father, who tells us this in his *Errors of the Profane Religions* (ch. XXIII):

> On a certain night [in March] an image is laid upon a bier, and it is mourned with solemn chants. When they are sated with this fictitious lamentation, a light is brought in. Then the mouths of all the mourners are anointed by a priest, who murmurs slowly: "Rejoice, followers of the saved god, because there is for you a relief from your grief."

Firmicus, sublimely unconscious of the image on a bier (or cross) or the fictitious lamentations of Good Friday, of the anointings and rejoicings of Easter morn, proceeds to ridicule his Mithraist rival:

> Thou dost bury an image, thou dost mourn an image, thou dost bring forth an image from the grave, and, wretched man, when thou hast done this, thou dost rejoice. . . . Thou dost arrange the members of the recumbent stone. . . . So the devil also has his Christs.

It is profound pity that the simple-minded Firmicus does not give us the full ritual. The weird and complicated ritual of the Catholic Church during Holy Week has probably borrowed scores of details from Mithraism.

Persia, and the entire sphere of influence of Persia, thus fall into line with the other nations. And here there is not the least trace of a phallic cult. The note is sin and salvation. Mithraism was as austere as Puritanism. Mithra was originally, not a fertility-god, but a sun-god. He had become the spiritual sun, the pattern of virtue, the savior from sin, the light of the world.

South of Byblus, in the great Phoenician city of Tyre, was another celebration that must not be omitted. The great god was Melcarth (commonly called Moloch), and a large effigy of him was solemnly burned every year. It is an obscure ceremony, but Josephus speaks of a festival at Tyre called "The Awakening of Hercules," and we may conclude that the burning of Melcarth was the equivalent of Hercules who, as we shall see, immolated himself on a funeral pyre, and ascended in a cloud to heaven.

From Tyre the Phoenicians, the great colonists and navigators, took their Melcarth over the seas. Carthage sent special envoys to the celebration in the mother-city every year. As far away on the coast of Spain, at Gades (Cadiz), which the Phoenicians founded, a great effigy of Melcarth was fired annually, and the god would rise again. Even in Tarsus of Cilicia—where Paul lived—there was a similar annual celebration.

Thus the old world elaborated its legends and bequeathed them to the new. The stream flowed on. But the Greek world, in which the new religion developed, had, besides temples and priests of every one of these older cults, very important myths of its own, and we must see these before we try to understand the meaning of this worldwide celebration.

5

Greek Resurrections

About two thousand years before Christ the pioneers of the Greek race reached the shores of the Mediterranean Sea and gazed with astonishment and delight on the blue waters and golden hills and islands. What were the precise features of the gods and goddesses they brought with them from the north, what still more primitive deities they adopted from the people whom they found already settled in Greece, how their poets and bards gradually enriched and transformed their early legends, it is difficult to say. But long before they became civilized, and borrowed the legends and cults of the older civilizations, they had myths of their own which aptly prepared them for the religion of Attis or Adonis or Christ. For some reason, which we will seek in the next chapter, the mind of man came in most parts of the world to conceive a legend of death and resurrection which your religious neighbor probably believes to be the unique property of his own Church.

Let me give one further illustration before we examine the Greek myths. When the Spanish priests crossed the seas to take the Catholic gospel to the "heathens" of Mexico, they were astonished to find that what seemed to them a caricature of it already existed in the country. There were austerities and atonements, monks and nuns, confession and communion, and many other remarkable anticipations of the wares they brought from Spain. "The devil has his Christs," they said, with old Firmicus Maternus. For us these resemblances throw a most interesting light on the evolution of religion. Thse Indians, starting from almost a polar district on the other side of the globe, isolated by vast spaces from the rest of the world, developed rites and beliefs singularly like those of ritualistic Buddhism in southern Asia and of Mithraism and Christianity in the region of the Mediterranean.

We have a relevant illustration of this in a spring-festival of the Aztecs which contains at least the germ of the death and resurrection myth. I may quote a description of it which I wrote a quarter of a century ago in my *Church Discipline:*

> About the beginning of April one of the finest of the war-prisoners at hand was chosen to represent the god. He was clothed in the resplendent robes of Tetzcatlipoca and awarded eight pretty pages and four of the mot charming maids of the community. He dined luxuriously, with the highest nobles of the land, and was in every way entertained as if he were the god he impersonated—for twenty days. On the last day of his reign his fair companions accompanied him on the royal canoe to the distant shore of the lake; and from the last kiss he turned with his pages toward the sinister temple beyond. The pages left him at the foot of the pyramid, and he mounted the solitary steps, playing the sacred flute. When he reached the summit, he was seized by the Aztec priests and flung upon the deep-stained altar; and in a few moments his sated heart was quivering before heaven in the outstretched hand of the sacrificer.

We find the same practice in other parts of the ancient world. In fact, in one form or other there was almost a worldwide belief that the god, or a representative (king, prisoner, effigy, etc.) of the god, died, or had to die, every year. Gods, being immortal in some sense, rise again when they die, so where the death of the god himself was celebrated, the feast of the resurrection followed. But for a poor war-captive or even a royal representative of the god there would be no resurrection.

In Greece we find various myths which bear upon this worldwide tendency of the human imagination. In some cases the legend as we have it is evidently modified by the contact of the Greeks with the oriental peoples, and for that we must make allowance. But two ancient myths, in particular, which became vital elements of Greek religious thought and life, familiarized the entire nation with the idea of a divine death and resurrection, a descent into hell and ascent into heaven; and these legends and the ritual they inspired reached the height of their popularity in the period before the spread of Christianity.

Zeus, the sky-father, the great god of the Greeks, corresponding to the Roman Jupiter, was mated with Hera (Juno). But in Greek mythology another matron-goddess, Demeter, is awkwardly placed on much the same level as Hera, and was much more popular. Most probably she is the customary mother-earth goddess of the people whom the Hellenes found in possession of Greece when they entered it. "Meter" is the Greek for "mother," and, although "De" is not the Greek for "earh" (which is "Ge"), it is probably the same word in an earlier tongue. We saw that in Crete, which influenced Greece before the Greeks arrived, the only deity was the mother-earth goddess; and scholars do not seem to have paid sufficient attention to the persistent statement of Greek writers that they got their "mysteries," originally, from Crete.

We will take it that the Greeks found this mother-goddess so deeply rooted in the mind of the people amongst whom they came that they had to admit her to the Olympic family. And Demeter had a daughter, Persephone, who also had to be admitted. They, of course, made her the daughter of Zeus by Demeter, and the wife of Pluto, the ruler of the world of the dead. But this "descent into hell" is the main point of interest for us.

The finished legend, as we find it in the seventh century B.C., says that Pluto fell in love with Persephone (also called Kore, or Cora, "the maid"). Zeus, always good-natured and very human, advised the god of the underworld to carry off the divine maid by force, as Demeter would never consent to her going below. So one day, as Persephone was gathering flowers in the celestial meadows, Pluto bore her away. Demeter searched the whole earth, in tears, for her daughter—as Isis had sought Osiris, as Ishtar had sought Tammuz, as the women sought Christ—and discovering where she was, nagged Zeus until he had to tell Pluto to give her up. Pluto agreed, but the desperate lover first induced Persephone to eat a pomegranate; and this, in Greek legend, made her a permanent citizen of the underworld. There was the usual compromise. Zeus said that she must pass one-third—later legend said one-half—of the year underground, and two-thirds with Demeter.

Mother and daughter, the spirit of love and vegetation and the queen of the dead, were honored with great and popular celebrations twice a year, at the time of sowing and the time of reaping. Out of or round these popular spring and harvest festivals—the two primeval festivals of the human calendar—developered the famous Greek "mysteries." But a mother alone, or even mother and daughter, cannot satisfy the heart. A son of god must sooner or later appear. Feminist writers might remind me that the development means that the primitive women-rule (matriarchate) of the world was at last invaded and superseded by the male; and, although it is now clear that there never was a universal matriarchate, there is, perhaps, a great deal of truth in the theory.

The divine son in Greece was Dionysus: known to the later Greeks and Romans as "Bacchus," which means "the noisy one" or "the rowdy one," the god of wine. Scholars believe that he was an old vegetation or fertility god in the barbarous country north of Greece, and was adopted by the Greeks. In their legends, however, they made him thoroughly Greek. He was the son of Zeus and the virgin Semele; and the phsyiology of these divine amours in Greek legend is such as to leave the mother a real virgin, so that Dionysus had a virgin birth. Hera, wife of Zeus, was angry, and the mother had to give birth in secret, in a cave, on a journey; and even then the child had to be sent far away to escape the vengeance of Herod—I mean Hera.

The goddess, however, had her revenge by visiting him in his early manhood with a kind of frenzy or insanity, and he wandered over the earth. He crossed rivers and lakes dry-foot, and he had other miraculous adventures. His character was twofold. On the one hand he introduced civilization everywhere: on the other, he introduced the wine and the frenzy of intoxication everywhere. There were two versions of his end. In one legend he descended into Hades, brought out his mother Semele, and with her ascended to heaven. In another he was cut to bits by the Titans, but was restored by Demeter, and rose from the dead, and ascended into heaven. At his birth-festival he was figured as a sweet divine babe in a basket-cradle, with the virgin mother Semele. Usually statues represented him as a handsome young god.

The "Dionysiac Mysteries," held in his honor, seem to have been wild meetings in commemoration of him as the god of wine and love, and do not concern us here. Respectable folk dismissed them as mere "orgies." The truth is that, as I have previously said, an ascetic and spiritual philosophy of life spread in Greece as well as Egypt and Babylonia before the time of Christ, and there were those who reacted upon it by having a candid celebration of "the flesh" and its delirious impulses.

The ascetics seem to have had a purified version of

this celebration in their "Orphic Mysteries." Orpheus does not interest us, but in the pageant there was a representation of the death and resurrection of Zagreus (a variant of Dionysus). He was torn to bits by the Titans, and at the prayer of his mother Persephone—whom some regarded as the mother of Dionysus—Zeus built a new Zagreus round the heart of the dead god which she brought to him.

But the "Eleusinian Mysteries" were the most famous, as Eleusis, where they were held, was only a few miles from Athens. In her wandering in search of her daughter, Demeter had sat by a well at Eleusis (as the woman of Samaria did) and had, unrecognized, been taken on at the royal court as a nurse, until it was found that she was turning the babe into an immortal. It is, of course, the same myth as that of Isis, and, as it is found in Greek literature in the seventh century, we cannot say which borrowed this detail from the other. We may conclude that Eleusis was one of the chief centers of the pre-Hellenic cult of the divine mother and daughter, and the Eleusinian Mysteries were in their honor. There were solemn processions from Athens, fasts to purify the worshipers, and long nocturnal ceremonies which included pageants of the birth of Iacchus (another variant of Dionysus) from Persephone, the mourning of the earth and Demeter when the young goddess descended into hell, and a rejoicing at her rise again into the world of the living.

These legends and celebrations, amongst the most famous and popular of the religious life of the time, made virgin births and resurrections as familiar as the day's events to every child of Hellas. And this was not all. More popular still was Heracles (or Hercules), the patron of hundreds of trade unions, the hero who rolled into one all the adventures of all the strong men, so that we still speak of a mighty task as "herculean."

Heracles had a virgin birth. His mother Alcmene was married, but, on account of a vow, still a virgin when

Zeus visited her, or the power of the Almighty overshadowed her. There was the usual threatening of the babe's life, and he had to be born in secret and hidden away. But the jealous Hera promised Zeus that she would lay aside her anger if the young demi-god would achieve twelve great works. These "labors of Hercules" do not interest us, but the end does. The wife of Heracles poisoned him, and he made a vat funeral pyre and got a shepherd to fire it. A cloud came down from heaven, and from the summit of the pyre Heracles was seen by his disciples to rise physically in the cloud to heaven; just as, hundreds of years later, it would be written of the virgin-born prophet of Nazareth that, from the summit of a hill, "he was taken up, and a cloud received him out of their sight." (Acts, i, 9).

Finally, in southern Greece there was another annual celebration, the Hyacinthia. Hyacinthus, youngest son of King Amyclas of Sparta, was so handsome that Apollo came down to play with him. And one day the god accidentally killed him as they played quoits. The hyacinth (a flower of the Greek spring, a small purple iris, not our hyacinth) sprang up out of his blood, and Apollo mourned bitterly. But we see from a bas-relief on his tomb at Amyclae that he ascended into heaven accompanied by a choir of divine nymphs. The annual celebration occupied three days. The first was given to mourning, the second to great joy, the third remains obscure. But it is the usual story. Some ancient god who was slain and rose again in the spring was adopted by the Greeks when they settled in Sparta. Resurrection was to the Greeks as familiar an idea as awakening in the morning. The Christian legend was not a piece of folly to them because it was impossible, but because it was banal. Aesculapius had raised so many from the dead that Zeus slew him lest the whole race of mortals should escape death; or, as others said, because Pluto found his lower world defrauded of crowds of its citizens. And Zeus had then raised Aesculapius himself from the dead and taken him into the company of the immortals. The Greeks, by the end of the old era, had come to realize that these were legends. And just then Paul of Tarsus came along to tell them that a god, a virgin-god, had really been slain recently in Judea and has risen from the dead! They laughed.

6

The Meaning of the Myth

In dealing with the myth of the virgin birth, we are apt to lose our judgment in this wonderful world of legends and religious fairy tales. If we find, as we do, a new religion appearing in the first century with a story of a slain and resurrected god, and we see clearly that such a story was current all over the world for ages before the first century, we are very prone to conclude at once that the new religion borrowed its story from the old ones.

That is not strictly logical. If, as we saw, the legend could grow up independently in four or five parts of the earth, it could appear independently in a sixth part. We say "grow up," but we must remember that legends are not like plants. They do not necessarily require a germ from a previous plant to engender them. The Greek (or pre-Greek), Phrygian, Persian, Egyptian, and Babylonian legends of death (or at least descent into the lower world) and resurrection arose independently. Why not the Christian? We rule out of court the Christian's claim that his story was quite independent because it is based upon a fact. The analysis of the evidence for it in the New Testament, which I made in the second chapter, demolishes that belief. There is only evidence that the belief existed amongst the followers of Jesus some years after his death.

But we must reflect before we say that the followers of Jesus merely borrowed what was said of other gods. The story of the resurrection as we have it in the Gospels seems very plainly to have been built up in part out of the older legends. We must, it is true, not strain the parallels and mythical interpretations. Conybeare, the chief Rationalist critic of the mythologists, seems to me justified in many of his criticisms. Jesus, they point out, was buried in a cave or rock-tomb. So was Mithra, therefore . . . Conybeare rightly points out that in stony Judea a man was generally buried in a rock-tomb. Again, it is said that Jesus walked on the water, and that he commandeered two asses on one occasion; and there is a legend that Dionysus once, to cross a river, commandeered one of two asses, and it walked on the water bearing him. It seems very doubtful [that] the ignorant writers of the Gospels knew that not very common legend; and the parallel is, in any case, very imperfect.

But the *finished* Christian story of the resurrection does seem to have been borrowed. The two days in the tomb are suspicious. The descent into hell is quite plainly pagan. The weeping women are very suggestive of borrowing. The ascent into heaven in a cloud is obviously borrowed from Heracles. And so on. As these things do not appear in the Christian story until after or about the end of the first century, there was plenty of time for the legend to pick up these bits of earlier stories. The early Christian who knew, for instance, that Heracles had risen to heaven in a cloud from the top of a high pyre before his disciples would not mind. "The devil has his Christs," he would say. It was an intelligent anticipation.

How far is it likely that the bald primitive story of the execution and resurrection of Jesus was borrowed? To me it seems that the crucifixion is probably historical: unless we reject the whole of Paul's Epistles. Paul, a few years after the event, living first among the Jews at Jerusalem—who never denied the crucifixion—could hardly be misled on such a point. The actual account of the "passion" is clearly a legendary expansion, but the death itself seems to be part of the human story of Jesus which the Jews, in their early conflict with the Christians, never questioned.

The question whether the early followers of Jesus then, within a few years of his death, borrowed the myth of the resurrection from other religions and applied it to him is not simple as some of the mythologists seem to suppose. Wherever Paul was "converted," he was won by the arguments of Jewish followers of Jesus in Judea; and, if we proceed on patient psychological and historical lines of inquiry, instead of bluntly rejecting the whole story, we have to ask how much the immediate and ignorant followers of Jesus knew about other slain and resurrected gods, and how far, if this knowledge were current in Judea, they would venture to appropriate and apply it. On the whole it seems more scientific and reasonable to suppose that, since the contemporary world was saturated with a resurrection myth, even Galilean fisherman knew something about it, and that the Messianic school held that the Messiah would rise from the dead. On the other hand, since the Gospels unanimously represent the disciples as dejected and scattered after the execution of their leader, and quite unwilling to believe in his resurrection—a point in favor of the historicity of the narrative, since later glorifiers of Jesus would hardly concoct such things—it seems clear that they did not then regard him as God.

Working on sober and patient lines, therefore, one is disposed to think that the disciples, or some of them, had come to believe that Jesus was the Messiah, without forming any theory of his divine nature, and that his execution shattered their belief for a time. Then there was the rally which we are accustomed to find in such circumstances. Possibly some of the women thought that they had, like Paul, subjective visions of Jesus; and such things could easily in a few years take objective form. I have traced modern miracles, both Catholic miracles at Lourdes and Spiritualist miracles, through five or six successive writers and copiers to the original documents, and it is curious to see how each amplifies or alters one word and omits others until the story looks quite different. Oral transmission of a story in the imaginative East, in a period of extreme nervous exaltation, would account for the simple story of the resurrection as it first appears in Paul. We have, as I said, no witnesses to the resurrection, so that the truth of the Christian belief is hardly worth discussing; but we have in some way to account for the belief itself. Later writers or Greek Christians could add mythical details, but it seems true neither to human nature nor to history to imagine the earliest Jewish followers of Jesus recalling that Mithra or Osiris had risen again and so saying that Jesus had done the same.

In sum, I should say that the universal belief in a slain and resurrected god throws light upon the Christian belief by showing us a universal frame of mind which quite easily, in many places, made a resurrection myth. We do not know how many of the obscure "Messiahs" who figure in Jewish history may have had the same or similar stories told of them. But none of them except Jesus had a Saul of Tarsus to spread his cult. But for that fiery and indomitable little man history would probably never have had to record the story of Christianity.

And Paul gave the new gospel its characteristic features: its ascetic and theological features. Jesus, an embodiment of God, died to save men from sin. The modern preacher stresses this aspect, and asks us to smile at all the stories of Osiris and the other slain and resurrected gods. The Christian story is a spiritual story, he says. Is it? In point of fact, the very bases of it are repugnant to the modern mind. If Jesus died to save men from sin, it was, as Paul says, from Adam's sin. On Christian principles the death of Christ does not atone for a man's personal sins. But only the less educated Christians now see anything "spiritual" in the idea that God condemned billions of human beings to eternal torment for the sin of one man. It is not spiritual, but sordid.

That was a mistake, of course, says the Modernist. Paul and everybody else were wrong—until the end of the nineteenth century. The real spiritual significance of the Christian story, its immense distinction from all other death and resurrection myths, is its moral inspiration. And the Modernist is in no better position than the Ancientists. As I have shown, the cult of Isis and Osiris in its latest form, the Greek Mysteries, and the cult of Mithra had exactly the same moral message. The celebration was a rebuke to sin, an exhortation to purity, a promise of personal resurrection. There is *nothing* unique in the Christian story. What is unique is the fact that of all the struggling cults of that wonderful age Christianity alone survived and conquered the world. I am now devoting a series of books to that. There is, we shall see, no more miracle or mystery in it than in all that we have yet surveyed.

But we are at the same time making a broad study of religious evolution, and a word must be said about the meaning of the general myth of a slain and resurrected god. It used to be thought that it was a fanciful allegory of the annual death (in winter) and restoration to life (in spring) of the sun. It is now more generally thought, with Sir J. G. Frazer, that the phenomenon on which the myth is based is the annual death and spring resurrection of the spirit of vegetation.

We have a natural tendency to make a single theory fit a large number of related facts, but in some cases it is a mistake. Here, in particular, we have *two* great facts— the decay and restoration of the sun and the decay and restoration of vegetation—in the actual order of nature, and some nations were more impressed by one than the other. The death and resurrection of Mithra, for instance, seems clearly a solar myth. The story of Demeter (mother earth) and her daughter just as clearly refers to vegetation; and the myth of Ishtar and Tammuz, Cybele and Attis, is equally clear. The myth of Isis and Osiris was a sun-god; but the evidence in Frazer and the time of the celebration (November) are against them.

The phenomena of nature's annual pageant are very different in different countries. To the northerner or the dweller on an elevated and temperate region the annual "slaying," or at least mortal illness, of the sun, which leads to the rigors of winter, is much more striking than the slow dying and slow rebirth of nature. To the southerner the waning of the sun in winter is rather a relief; while most of the vegetation is dead during the greater part of the year, and it is the sudden and glorious burst of flowers and corn that impresses. So we get both solar and vegetation myths, and combinations of the two, and, as the season of rain and growth varies considerably, we find the celebration at different times of the year.

But what a consummation! Man in his childhood speculates on the annual pageant of nature. What does it mean? Mother-earth and father-sky never die. They are always there. But the spirit of the sun and the spirit of the corn and tree die or sicken every year, and rise again. Or perhaps they merely pass for a season to the underworld? Man weaves his fairy tales about the great pageant. The son of God or the daughter or lover of earth is slain, or dies, or is dragged to the underworth every year. We mourn with mother-earth; we rejoice in the restoration.

Then the ideas of sin and virtue enter. They come to be regarded as conditions of one's immortal lot. The life beyond had at first been conceived merely as an eternal duplicate of this. The death and resurrection festivals were more or less in the nature of religious magic. They were to promote fertility; and love and feasting promote fertility. Now the drama becomes ethical. The next world is purely spiritual, and you must not go into it with sin on your soul. The robust and wicked old celebrations become "mysteries." At last, by a curious chain of historical accidents, an old Sumerian myth of a fall of man enters the story. The god really dies to atone for the race; and for two thousand years nearly the whole race pretends to shudder in the shadow of the cross. It is fast fading from the earth, in spite of a hundred thousand priests. The pageant of nature has a new interpreter: science. The pageant of religions has a new interpreter: history. We discard myths and legends. We chart our way in the light of new knowledge and the strength of a new consciousness.

Did Jesus Ever Live?

1

The Modern Denial

The Little Blue Books which I have written on the origin of religion, the revolt against it, and phases of morals, form an indispensable historical introduction to the study of Christ and Christianity.

The version of the religious history of mankind which the Christian usually cherishes is pathetically inaccurate. Human reason, he thinks, feels a certain magnetic force, a religious instinct, which directs it toward the Pole Star of the universe: God. But the base metals of the earth distract and confuse it. In its vagaries it points in a hundred directions. It frames a thousand religions. At last God, who contemplates these pitiful and futile wanderings during three thousand years of civilization, and some tens of thousands of years of prehistoric life, gives a partial revelation of himself through the prophets of one of the smallest nations on the earth. It does not suffice; and then God takes human form, and brings the full blaze of truth to man. And the nations fall upon their knees, and turn from sin and error to virtue and knowledge.

This is as false in every syllable as was the astronomy of the Chaldeans or the natural history of the Middle Ages.

Man has no religious instinct. His early creeds are

artless deductions from things which he does not understand. When the dull eye of the primitive savage kindles at last with some speculations, nature seems to him to be a great puppet show, worked by mysterious powers behind the scenes. How still, how lifeless, it can be on a calm moonlit night or in the depth of winter! Then the sun rises, or the spring comes, and a thousand energies awaken. Spirits or gods animate the dead frame of nature, he concludes.

With higher social organization and larger ideas and more ambitious priesthoods man comes to believe that one great power vitalizes the whole of nature. This advance may be due mainly to the monopolizing tendency of priests, which make Aten in Egypt, Marduk in Babylon, or Jahveh in Palestine, the one God: or it may be philosophers like Pythagoras or Plato who seriously reason that matter is "dead" and the life in it must come from a cosmic power beyond it. In any case, this monotheistic creed appears, quite naturally, ages before any Hebrew prophet even claimed a revelation. At the same time but independently, higher ideals of divine and human conduct are developed. *Every great civilization on the earth attained an ethical spiritual monotheism long before Jesus was born.* We have proved that.

In those circumstances Jesus is no phenomenon, no miracle, but one of the most natural events of his time; and not an uncommon event. I am for the moment considering Jesus as described in the Gospels. No one knows exactly where they were written, but they certainly appeared within a definitely limited territory: that is to say, in one or other of the cities on the coast of the Mediterranean where the dispersed Jews mingled with Greeks, Persians, and Egyptians.

In other booklets I give the reader the material for forming a picture of that region nineteen hundred years ago. It was the center of the civilized world: the fringe at which the Greco-Roman world overlapped with the Egyptian-

Babylonian-Persian: one of the most cosmopolitan regions that ever existed, particularly in regard to religion.

A map of this wonderful region, as it then was, lies before me; and I brood over it until I seem to be high above it, in some magical airplane, watching the seething life of its cities. At the southern corner of this great blue bay of the Mediterranean is Alexandria. All the knowledge and idealism of venerable Egypt have settled there; and they are blended with all the knowledge and idealism of the Greeks. It is the world's most famous center of learning and religion. There are splendid schools and austere monasteries. The cross is a familiar symbol; and priests of Isis, with shaven polls and fine linen garments, sprinkle holy water on penitents. Every year there are solemn celebrations of the miraculous birth of the divine son of the virginal Kore or of the semi-virginal Isis, and of the resurrection of a god, Osiris, who is to judge the living and the dead.

Along the coast of Palestine are half a dozen smaller cosmopolitan cities. In ancient Tyre and Sidon, in Gaza and Ptolemais, the cultures of the Egyptians, Cretans, Babylonians, Persians, Hittites, Phoenicians, Phrygians, Hebrews, and Greeks mingle. Temples rise in scores; and a score of rival priesthoods shriek their wares to the multitude. "Come and be saved from your sins," is the common cry. Here the cult of the Phoenician slain and resurrected God, Adonis, meets his counterpart from Phrygia (Athis), from Babylonia (Tammuz), and from Egypt (Osiris). Here the new Persian religions of austerity and repentance, Mithraism and Manicheism, bring a new miraculously born savior and a new judge of the living and the dead; and they are as stern about sin and repentance as the most bilious spinster could desire.

But if the oriental sun is still in your blood, if you think love a gift of the gods, there is Byblus wit its beautiful temple of impurity, Antioch with its enchanted pleasures, and, a short sail over the water, Paphos with its undying odor of roses and blaze of sensuality.

Further north are Tarsus (where a fiery little tent-maker broods on these things) and Seleucia. Further west, following the bend of the coast, are Rhodes and Laodicaea, Ephesus and Smyrna, Corinth and Athens, and heaven knows how many other cosmopolitan cities, where the latest Stoic moralists and argumentative Jews and Asiatic and Egyptian evangelists fill the air with cries of sin, repentance, and of the world, judgment, baptism, mortification of the flesh, virtue, spirituality, the true god, resurrection, immortality, and so on, and so on.

What, in the name of common sense, could Jesus or anybody else add to all this? There were hundreds of Jesuses. A life of the Rabbi Hillel, if we had one suitably embroidered with miracles, would be a life of Jesus. A life of the slave-moralist, Epictetus, if we had one, would be a perfect life of Jesus. The life which we have of the wandering apostle Apollonius of Tyana is a life of Jesus. The chief teachings, even the phrases and sentiments to a great extent, were common to priests of Isis, Serapis, Esmun, Apollo, Mithra, Ahura-Mazda, and Jahveh, as well as wandering Stoic apostles.

Every single moral sentiment attributed to Christ in the Gospels has several parallels in the literature of the time. There is not one point in the "teaching of Christ" that was new to the world. Even the parables were borrowed from the Jewish Rabbis. The chief doctrinal features of the Christ of the Gospels—the birth, death, and resurrection—were familiar myths at the time, and were borrowed from "the pagans."

What we see, in fact, is evolution in religion. The ideas pass on from age to age, a mind here and a mind there adding or refining a little. The slow river of human evolution had entered its rapids. The mingling of twenty nations in a series of world-empires had brought about such a clash of ideas as the world had never seen since until our time. Every possible shade of moral idealism and religious thought was represented, from Alexandria to Rome. You could blot Christ out of the history of the first three centuries of the "Christian Era"—what happened after that is a different matter, as we shall see in due time—and it would make no more difference than cutting a single tree out of a well-wooded landscape.

Blot out Christ! Yes, that is what many serious scholars are now attempting to do, and we must consider that first. It is, to the Rationalist, to any man who resents this long distraction of the race by the Christian religion, a tempting proposition. Suppose we could prove that there never had been on this earth such a person as Jesus! What an ironic consummation! Yet this modern denial is so weighty that we find so cautious and courtly an authority as Sir J. G. Frazer writing, in *Enigma of Jesus,* that "whether Dr. Couchoud be right or wrong" in denying the historicity of Jesus, "he appears to have laid his finger on a weak point in the chain of evidence on which hangs the religious faith of a great part of civilized mankind."

The highest authority in this field is my learned friend the Right Honorable J. M. Robertson, an English Privy Councillor. In the year 1795 a French professor, Dupuis, of the Revolutionary school, published a large work (*The Origin of All Cults*) in which he attempted to trace all religious beliefs to astronomical myths; and the gospel Jesus was thus dissolved away with all other gods. For a time in the nineteenth century this solar-myth, or astronomical, theory of religion was very popular. It has a certain fascination; and there is in fact a very great deal of astronomical speculation in religion. Sky-gods and sun-gods are very common; and to some extent, at least, the legend of the annual dying of a god and rebirth or resurrection is based upon the solar phenomena of winter and spring. But, like so many theories, the solar-myth interpretation of religion was pressed too far, and it fell out of favor.

In 1835, however, the famous German Rationalistic

theologian, Strauss, published a fresh attempt to dissolve the Gospel Jesus into myths (*Life of Jesus*), and his very learned work made a serious impression. But Strauss, as Mr. Robertson says, explained away only part of the "figure of Jesus" and "left all the rest utterly problematical."

Mr. Robertson took up the subject several decades ago and came to the conclusion that no such historical person as Jesus ever existed. In a long series of very learned works (*Christianity and Mythology, Pagan Christs*, etc.) he has attempted to show that nearly every important detail in the life of Christ is mythical, and is very largely astronomical myth. Jesus, he holds, was an obscure deity amongst the later Jews, and these myths were gradually fitted to him and turned into actual human events. The birth, death, and resurrection are an obvious illustration. The birth is the annual rebirth of the sun; the death and resurrection legends are another conception of the sun's winter-death and spring-triumph over death.

In particular, Mr. Robertson holds that the entire story of the crucifixion and what preceded it is merely a description of a sacred drama which was obscurely presented annually in Judea. Just as some nations in Europe now make an annual "Passion Play" (at Oberammergau, etc.) out of the Gospel narrative, so originally the Gospel narrative was made out of a Passion Play, or sacred drama, or "mysteries." For instance, Matthew (xxvi 39, etc.) describes the words of Christ's prayer in the garden of Gethsemane while his disciples were asleep (so that nobody really heard them). But that, Mr. Robertson points out, is just how a spectator would describe a drama; and other details suggest the same.

I do not think Mr. Robertson has given us sufficient historical reason to believe that such a play was found among the Jews. It is difficult to believe that such a play was found among the Jews. It is difficult to believe, and I see no reason or need to believe it. No Jewish writer hints at such a thing. It seems to me also that a great deal of Mr. Robertson's analysis of details of the gospels into myths is strained and improbable. Another Rationalist, a learned teacher at Oxford University, Mr. F. C. Conybeare, has attacked Mr. Robertson's theory on these grounds (*Myth, Magic, and Morals* and *The Historical Christ*), and his criticisms are impressive. In fine, it seems most unlikely that the Jews had a pre-Christian deity named Jesus (an ordinary proper name in its Jewish form), and none of these critical writers gives adequate evidence of the existence of such a deity.

Professor W. B. Smith of Tulane University, another writer (though his specialty is philosophy) who denies the historicity of Jesus, makes, perhaps, the most learned attempt to show that he was a pre-Christian deity turned by his followers into an historical human being. In his *Ecce Deus* he exposes, in the usual way, the feebleness of the evidence for the historicity of Jesus, shows that much of the detail is mythical, and very acutely criticizes the contradictions and uncertainties of the liberal theologians who try to give us a human life of Christ. But when one seeks evidence, apart from the Gospels themselves, that there ever was such a deity as Jesus, it is not forthcoming. Professor Smith simply insists that Jesus was a god of the Gnostic sects and is so described in the gospels; that, to their Gnostic readers, the gospels did not even profess to tell an historical human story, but to speak symbolically.

The third leading writer of the school is the German Professor Drews, whose *Witnesses to the Historicity of Jesus* I translated into English. That book is mainly concerned with the supposed evidence for the historicity, which we will examine. But in it and other works Professor Drews holds that Jesus is a deity who was gradually turned into a human being by his followers; and that astronomical myth has provided a great deal of the material.

The latest writer is Dr. P. L. Couchoud, of Paris, to the English translation of whose *Enigma of Jesus* Sir J. G.

Frazer (while dissenting from the main conclusion) writes a flattering introduction. Dr. Couchoud starts from his medical experience of neurotic and exalted patients, and he concludes that Jesus is an imaginary spiritual being or deity born only in the minds of certain Jews during a mystical revival. Prosper Alfaric (in an article in the *Revue historique,* January, 1924), Vittorio Macchioro (*Zagreus* and *Orfismo* and *Paolinismo*), and a few other scholars have joined in the same conclusion; that Jesus was a mythical being or deity whose followers gradually gave him human shape.

We cannot here analyze all these large and learned works, but in the following chapters we will consider their main arguments. The three chief considerations in the minds of all writers who deny the historicity of Christ are: (1) that the Gospels are totally unreliable as history; (2) that Paul bears no witness to a human Jesus; and (3) that pagan and Jewish writers are singularly silent about the Prophet of Nazareth. These points we will examine, and then we may be in a position to come to some conclusion.

2

The Fiction of the Gospels

The less learned of the clergy pour fine scorn on this modern denial of the historicity of Jesus. It is a humorous illustration, they say, of the extravagances of the spirit of denial. There is a legend amongst them that an archbishop once showed that on the same principles you could prove that Napoleon I never existed: which certainly would be a humorous thing to do, as there were plenty of people still living in the archbishop's time who had actually seen Napoleon! I have myself known old ladies who remembered his death.

The ordinary believer is startled by, and is apt to be impatient of, the very question which forms the title of this book. But a very little reflection, if he will condescend to it, will show him that it is a quite serious question. A number of characters whose historical existence was as certain as the sun to whole ages—King Arthur, Homer, William Tell, etc.—have proved to be legendary. Adam is certainly a legend: Moses and Abraham are most probably legends: Zarathustra is doubtful. If the historicity of Jesus is so very certain, there must be some quite indisputable witnesses to it. Who are they?

The Gospels. Now, just as science is said to be "organized common sense," so modern scientific history organizes or directs common sense in these matters. Who wrote the Gospels? No one knows. They are entitled "According to Matthew," etc., not "by Matthew," etc., in the oldest Greek manuscripts and in early references to them. Indeed, as we saw in *The Forgery of the Old Testament,** even if they professed to be written by Matthew, etc., it would not follow that they were. But they do not profess this. Many scholars think, on very slender grounds, that the third Gospel was actually written by Luke. We shall see; though it matters little for our purpose, as the writer expressly says that he was not an eyewitness. He is, he says (i, 1–3), writing down for a friend, as "many" others have done before him, and account of what they have *heard* about Jesus.

What we want to know about the Gospels is whether the men who wrote them were in a position to know the facts. In ordinary history we ask two questions about any writer: what was his knowledge of the facts, and is he truthful? In dealing with religious documents, especially Oriental documents, we have to be particularly critical. Let me illustrate this.

About twenty years ago Mr. Myron H. Phelps wrote an account (*Life and Teachings of Abbas Effendi*) of the origin of the new Babi or Behai religion which was then finding adherents in America. It arose out of the teaching of a *Persian* reformer, Ali Mohammed, called "the Bab" (gate). Like Christ, but in the year 1844 A.D., Ali Mohammed set out to reform the accepted creed and to bring people back to the worship of a purely spiritual God. He and hundreds of his followers were put to death, in 1850, by a combination of Persian priests and government; and what Sir J. G. Frazer calls "the bribe of immortality" had no place in the faith of those fearless martyrs. But the significant point is this: two or three years after the death

*Little Blue Book No. 1066

of the Bab his life was written, and it was a purely human account of a Christ-like man; but some decades later a new life appeared richly embroidered with miracles in the Gospel manner!

What happened in the east in the nineteenth century could, surely, happen in the first century. If these lives of Jesus, the Gospels were not written until some decades after his death, we must read them with great caution. The American Fundamentalist, who is the last to realize this, ought to be the first. He knows well how Catholic enthusiasm still makes miracles at Lourdes and St. Anne. Enthusiasm even innocently, always glorifies its cause with miralces. In the early days of Spiritualism an eminent British judge published some remarkable experiences he had had a few years before; and he was compelled, in great confusion, to admit that his memory was entirely wrong and he had misstated the facts in every important detail.

It is therefore most important to know when the Gospels were written. If they were not written until several decades after the death of Christ—if the stories about Christ passed merely from mouth to mouth in an Oriental world for a whole generation at least after his death— it is neither reasonable nor honest to put implicit faith in them. There were no journals in those days. Few people could read and write. Moreover, the Jews were scattered over the earth by the Romans in the year 70 A.D.; and the Christians had previously been scattered by the Jews themselves. What should we make of a story going from mouth to mouth in such conditions as these for several decades?

However, let us approach the subject on common-sense lines. How are we to test whether the writers of the Gospels knew the facts and did not merely put on parchment what was being said in the obscure and scattered Christian communities? Some Christian writers try to apply what are called internal tests. They say that the description of places and customs and daily life in Judea is so confident and precise in the Gospels that the writers were evidently familiar with the country in the time of Christ.

Tests of this kind are very delicate and uncertain. In one of Mr. H. G. Wells' novels—*Marriage*, I think—the story is partly located in Labrador, which is minutely and accurately described. I found that few people had any doubt but that Wells had been there. But, when the able novelist was writing that book, he told me that he had just collected all the available books on Labrador and was "steeping himself" in the subject. He has never been near Labrador. Similarly, Prescott, the vivid American historian of the conquest of Mexico and Peru, never saw either land. He was blind.

A careful writer can easily "get up" a country in this way. Keeping common sense as our guide, however, we will not suppose that a number of early Christians "got up" Galilee and Judea in order to write lives of Jesus. In point of fact, they have only a very general and often inaccurate knowledge. *Mark* is generally admitted to be oldest Gospel, and it is by no means detailed and precise in topography. In others, such as *Luke*, there are historical errors. *Luke* admittedly did *not* know Judea.

But we need not linger over tests of this sort. Take the book of *Daniel*. It is as vivid and precise and circumstantial as any Gospel; and it is quite demonstrably a forgery written centuries after the time it describes. We should say the same of a very great deal of the Old Testament. Such tests are useless. They would break down hopelessly in "Homer." They would prove that Dante had really visited hell. They would make Keats a native of Corinth.

The first condition of any confidence in the Gospels is to ascertain that the writers lived within a reasonable time of the events described; and one hundred and fifty years of biblical scholarship have not succeeded in finding any proof of that. At present the general opinion is that

Mark, the oldest Gospel, was written between 65 and 70 A.D.; and *Matthew* and *Luke* in the last decade of the first century; and *John* in the second century. *Mark,* it will be remembered, knows nothing about the miraculous birth of Christ; the first account of that turns up at least ninety years after the supposed event!

Moreover, the resurrection story and other details are not supposed, and cannot be proved by anybody, to have been in *Mark* by the year 70. Scholars have come to the conclusion that there existed at first a simple sketch of the life of Jesus which is the groundwork of the first three Gospels (and is best seen in Mark) and a collection of teachings which is most used by *Matthew.* At what date this sketch was written nobody knows. What precisely was in it nobody knows. You cannot put your finger on a single verse and say that it is part of the *original* Gospel. And, even if you could, there is not a scrap of evidence that it was written within thiry years of the death of Christ. Remember Ali Mohammed and his miracles!

If a religious reader thinks that he can dismiss all this as "Higher Criticism stuff," and points out how much these critics have changed their theories and how contradictory they are, let him reflect on his own position. He trusts the Gospels without any evidence whatever; without making the least inquiry into their authority. His preachers dogmatically say that the Gospels were "inspired"—though the opening verses of *Luke* plainly say the contrary—and he takes their word as simply as a child does.

This "Higher Criticism," which he hears so much reviled, is a very serious and conscientious effort of Christian divines, sustained now for more than a hundred years, to prove that the Gospels are worthy of ordinary historical credence. It has failed. The miraculous birth, the death on the cross, the resurrection and ascension, and the healing miracles, it is compelled to sacrifice altogether. By great effort it then concludes that some sort of small Gospel or life of Jesus was in existence thirty years after the death of Christ; but that is too late to be reliable, and no one knows exactly what it said.

Moreover, while there is no evidence at all that the Gospels, our Gospels, existed before the end of the first century, there is very serious evidence that they did not. *No Christian writer mentions one of our four Gospels until a hundred years after the death of Christ or makes any clear and certain quotation from any one of them.* That is serious, surely. Yes, you may say, if it is true; but it may be another bit of Higher Criticism or of Rationalism. It is not. It is the very serious verdict of a committee of historians and divines appointed to study this question by the Oxford (University) Society of Historical Theology, an ecclesiastical society. They courageously published this disappointing result of their labors in *The New Testament in the Apostolic Fathers* (1905).

Pope St. Clement of Rome, for instance, wrote an important letter, which we have, about 96 A.D.; and a second letter bearing his name, though probably a Christian forgery, was written later. About the same time, or a little earlier, there were the so-called *Epistle of Barnabas* and the first part of the *Teaching of the Apostles*. These never quote from, or refer to, the Gospels. For the first three decades of the second century we have the second part of the *Teaching*, the *Pastor* (supposed to be by "Hermas"), and letters of Bishops Ignatius and Polycarp. Not one of these mentions the Gospels or makes a clear quotation from them. They quote certain words which roughly correspond to words in *Matthew, Luke,* and (at a late date) *John;* but this proves nothing, as by the second century these sayings of Christ certainly circulated in the Church. We must say the same of the *Sayings of Our Lord* (or *Logia*), a second-century fragment containing seven "sayings," two of which are in the Gospels. It has no significance whatever, unless it be to discredit the Gospels. The writer clearly knew of no Gospel collections.

It is not until about 140 or 150 A.D. that Christian writers refer to and quote from the Gospels. They are clearly known to Justin, Marcion, and Papias. The latter, the Bishop of Herapolis, an ignorant and credulous man who writes a good deal which nobody now believes, is known to us only from quotations in the fourth-century historian Eusebius; a man who notoriously held that the use of statements to the Church was more important than their accuracy. This fourth-century quotation of a second-century obscure bishop is the only "serious" evidence for the Gospels! Papius says that he learned from older men that Mark and Matthew really wrote Gospels. That is not evidence that any historian would credit, and, in fact, divines do not believe it.

In order to realize the full significance of this, it is necessary to know a little more about the early Christian world than a Christian usually knows. He imagines just a loyal group of virtuous men and women meeting secretly here and there, at Corinth or Ephesus or Thessalonica, to break bread and pray to Jesus. On the contrary, from about 50 to 150 A.D., early Christianity was a most intense ferment of contradictory speculations. Greek, Persian, Jewish, Egyptian, and all kinds of religious ideas were blended with Christianity. We know the names of at least a score of Christian intellectual leaders and sects of the time. Gradually, of course, these people were thrust outside the Church and called "Gnostics"; but in the first century and the early part of the second Christian communities everywhere swarmed with these mystics.

It was in such a world that the Gospels gradually took shape. The idea of the average believer, that someone sat down one day and, under inspiration, wrote a "Gospel according to Matthew," and so on, is naively unhistorical. The writer of Luke indicates what happened. For decades the faithful merely talked about Christ. Men like Paul went from group to group, much as the cheapest types of revivalists do today, and talked about Jesus. Probably few of them could read, in any case; and Paul, to judge by his Epistles, had very little to say about an earthly life of Jesus. Then, here and there, some who could write put upon parchment what was being said. All sorts of wild and contradictory stories about Jesus were going about. Our four Gospels are just four that were selected in the fourth century out of a large number. These little biographies and lists of "sayings" grew larger and larger. There was no central authority to check them; the various communities were a day's or even a week's journey apart; and travel was costly for poor folk. There was not the slightest approach to what we call standardization.

So it is mere waste of time to write a Life of Jesus by a sort of intelligent selection of what you think is probable in the Gospels. All the Rationalist and other such biographies, from Strauss and Renan to Papini, are just subjective compilations. You may think it probable that Jesus really did this or that, but you cannot call it an historical fact because it is in the Gospels. The figure of Jesus, the biography, grew, as time went on. And, since that growth took place, during at least half a century of unchecked speculation and argumentation, in a world of Oriental mysticism and theosophy, you see the strength of the writers who hold that Jesus (as many of the Gnostics held) never was a man at all.

3

Paul and Jesus

Dining one night with George Moore, and discussing Jesus, I told him how I thought that Jesus was an Essenian monk. Moore, who professes genially to be a "Protestant"—solely because he hates Catholicism—was more interested in Paul. But, like the great artist he is, he saw the value of my suggestion, and a little later appeared his literary drama, *The Apostle.* It was rather too dramatic—Paul in the end meets Jesus in a monastery and kills him, when he finds that Jesus did not really die and rise again—and Moore asked me to go with him to Palestine and make a serious study. I, unfortunately, could not go, but Moore did, and out of it came his finest work, *The Brook Kerith:* which is nearer to the truth than any Life of Jesus or learned theological volume on the Gospels.

Paul was the real founder of Christianity, on the small scale on which it existed during the first three centuries. Ambrose, we shall see, was the founder of later, or ecclesiastical, Christianity. Paul was a Pharisee, and the Gospel pictures of the Pharisees mislead most believers. You see them in illustrated Bibles as richly dressed, haughty men, the heavy hems of whose robes poor folk must not touch. Most of them had, like Paul, no robes to speak of. Three-fourths of the Jews of the time—the great mass of the workers and farmers—were Pharisees. The New Testament writers hated them for their loyalty to the Jewish law and calumniated them.

The whole world was, as I said, then discussing religion. Every historic creed was in the melting pot, and new creeds rose in the pot like bubbles. Paul, or Saul, was a fiery little man, a working man, like (except in ability) hundreds that you will see any day in the fringe of open-air meetings. And all his fierce disputing ended in his accepting Jesus. It may very well have been during a journey to Damascus. Men of this type easily saw visions in the east: they do even in Pittsburgh today.

But the *Acts of the Apostles* is as feeble historically as the Gospels, and we will not try to construct a story of Paul. We know him well from his Epistles. "The style is the man," said Buffon. Paul's style is Paul. It is as characteristic as the style of Anatole France, or Maeterlinck, or G. B. Shaw. Well, some years after the supposed date of the death of jesus this strong-headed enthusiast began to believe in him. What kind of Jesus did he accept? What testimony does he bear to Christ?

First, who is going to assure us that the Epistles of Paul are themselves genuine? It is foolish of believers to resent these perpetual questions. Nothing was thought in those days of putting a respected name on your essay or epistle. Early Christian literature includes a number of spurious Epistles and Gospels. And, since Paul's style is so characteristic, the ordinary apparatus of literary criticism enables us to say that some of the Epistles which bear his name were not written by him. They have not the same style and ideas.

This does not matter so very much for my purpose, but I will take those Epistles of which Professor Drews admits the genuineness. He says that in these Paul never refers to Jesus as a human being: that his Jesus is a deity only, whom later Christians supposed to have lived on earth at one time: that the apparent references to earthly experiences are really quotations of the things attributed to the Messiah in the prophets.

It seems to me that the whole argument of Professor Drews, Professor Smith, and others breaks down before one statement which runs from end to end of Paul's Epistles: the emphatic statement that Christ died on a cross and rose from the dead, and that this is the very basis of faith in him. It is little use recalling that Osiris or Tammuz rose from the dead. Ignorant Egyptians could believe that a god, as such, had a body, which could be killed. To a man like Paul such an idea would seem monstrous. He distinguishes quite clearly between God and Jesus. God, a purely spiritual being, takes human shape in Jesus, and sheds his blood on a cross, is buried, and then, in human shape, comes to life again. I do not see how anybody not obsessed by a theory can fail to recognize that, less than ten years after the alleged crucifixion of Jesus, Paul fully accepted that part of his story. "Being found in fashion as a man, he humbled himself, and became obedient unto death, even the death of the cross." (*Phil.* ii 8). With infinite variations of expression, that formula is found in every Epistle, and it is Paul's fundamental belief about Jesus.

Now this single statement carries us a very long way. No one has ever suggested that Paul had any doubt about the divinity of Jesus. It would follow, though Paul merely says that Jesus was "born of a woman," that he accepted some sort of miraculous story about the actual birth and childhood of this God in human shape. He refers repeatedly, in all Epistles, to Cephas or Peter and other Jews who boasted of some superior mission to his, because they had seen and known the Lord. He represents that Jesus preached and taught in Judea. In one place (*I Cor.* ix 14) he quotes as a saying of the Lord something ("They which preach the gospel should live by the gospel") which *Matthew* (x 10) and *Luke* (x 7) give, in other words, as the actual teaching of Jesus. He says nothing plainly about healing miracles; but is it likely that Paul believed Jesus to be God himself in human form and did not credit him with signs and wonders as he went about Judea? Finally, there is a passage (*I Tim.* vi 13) in which he speaks of his trial before Pontius Pilate: there are a hundred passages in which he says that Jesus was crucified, and by the Jews (*I Thess.* ii 15): and there are a thousand references to his physical resurrection.

We may put aside as spurious or interpolated such isolated statements as that the Christian supper is founded upon the actual last supper of Christ (*I Cor.* x 16 and xi 23-26): though no one will doubt that there was such a supper among the earliest Christians. We many similarly set aside the isolated references to Pontius Pilate, to Peter's claim to have seen Jesus after the resurrection, and to the ascension (*Eph.* ix 10). But there remains one unshakable story about Jesus which is found in every single Epistle. I run over them and for the convenience of the reader indicate these passages, one or more in every Epistle: *Rom.* i 3-4, iv 24, v and vi in full, etc.; *I Cor.* x 16, xi 23-6, xv, etc; *II Cor.* iv 10; *Gal.* i 4, iv 4, vi 14; *Eph.* i 7, 20, etc.; *Philipp.* ii 8; *Coloss.* i 20, 22, etc.; *I thess.* i 10, ii 15; *I Tim.* vi 13; *II Tim.* i 10, ii 18, etc.; *Titus* ii 4-6; *Hebr.* i 2-3, ii 9, ix 14, etc.

It is, therefore, no use (from our present point of view) arguing that this or that Epistle is not genuine. Unless we follow the eccentric opinion of Van Manen, and say that they are all spurious, Paul bears definite witness to Jesus. He lived on earth, in Judea, for at least two or three decades; because he was "born of a woman," yet lived to be a teacher. He was put to death on a cross by the Jews; and it was an article of faith with his followers that he rose from the dead. Just as consistently, from end to end, Paul repeats the assurance of Jesus that the end of the world is at hand, and the Lord will judge the living and the dead.

Farther, the Epistles uniformly and entirely depict the early Christian world in a manner which must interest us. Paul's great period of activity was from about 45 to 65 A.D. Let us say that the Epistles were mainly written between 50 and 60 A.D. There were then groups of believers in Jesus, on the same lines as Paul, in every large center from Jerusalem to Rome. Many of them were old enough to have lost their first fervor, and he describes them as much given to fornication. His persistence and emphasis also indicate that there is some reluctance to believe in the resurrection, which is, he says, "foolishness to the Greeks"—thus clearly showing that he means a physical resurrection. The little "churches" or communities are full of dissensions, but they are not on Gnostic lines. They are about the Jewish law, the way in which Christ saves from sin, the resurrection, and the question of authority. There is repeated reference to a group of men, chiefly Cephas, who are described as the living companions and appointed apostles of Jesus. Their center is Jerusalem. They are intensely Jewish and have many a fiery conflict with Paul.

The witness of Paul is, then, that from about 40 A.D. to 60 A.D. there were, scattered over the Greco-Roman world, small groups of followers of Christ, and they were visited occasionally by Jews who had, they claimed, known Jesus in the flesh and received instruction from him. They all believed that he was the Son of God, who had assumed a human form and died on a cross to atone for the sins of men. This atonement by *blood* was of the very essence of their faith. It was the common idea of the time in the east that bloody sacrifice was the best atonement for sin, and it was a magnificent idea to some of these mystic Orientals that God himself should take human form and become a human sacrifice. To work out that belief they had to give God two aspects (which later theology would call "persons"), Father and Son; but Jewish religion had already plenty of references to Sons of God, and Greek mysticism also spoke of a Logos of God.

We will see later what this witness of Paul proves—
if it proves anything. For the moment it is enough to
establish that Paul *does* believe in the human historicity of Christ. He never ceases to repeat that Jesus was
a teacher in Judea, who died on the cross and rose from
the dead. The condescension of God in taking human form,
the shedding of real human blood in the ignominious punishment of the cross, are the quintessence of his gospel.
The Jesus of Paul was a divine human person, who was
put to death at Jerusalem somewhere about 30 A.D.

4

Jewish and Pagan Witnesses

On the very day on which I begin to write this little book
(May 30, 1926), the leading Sunday newspaper of Britain,
the *Observer,* has a prominent article on "Jesus Christ
in History." The pretext of it—a claim that new evidence
has been found—I will discuss presently; but a part of
the article must have surprised many people.

The writer is an orthodox and respected English theologian, Dr. Burch. He is going to publish a book about
this supposed new evidence for the historicity of Jesus.
Meantime, as his publishers naturally will not allow him
to give away the great secret, he writes articles in connection with it.

In this article he deals with "the scantiness of references to Christ in the histories which have come down
to us." He quotes "the ablest Jewish book on the whole
subject," Klausner's recent *Jesus of Nazareth;* and he shows
that, in the way of non-biblical witnesses to Christ, we
have only "twenty-four lines" from Jewish and pagan
writers, and four of those are spurious. Of the twenty
genuine lines twelve (which are almost universally regarded as spurious) are in the Jewish historian Josephus.
In the immense Latin literature of the century after the

death of Jesus there are only eight lines; and each of these is disputed.

Certainly a disturbing silence from the Christian point of view. We might argue that, since the Jews were very hostile to the Christians, their great writers, Philo and Josephus, would be not unnaturally reluctant to speak about them. We might suggest that the teaching and crucifixion of Jesus , more than a thousand miles away from Rome, in a very despised province, would not be likely to come even to the notice of a Roman writer. Yet how strange, how ironic, that God should have lived on earth, for the salvation of men, during thirty years, and consummated a great sacrifice which dwarfs every other event in human history, and the stream of literature can flow on for a hundred years without more than half a dozen disputed lines on these transcendent miracles!

In these little works we are trying to take a common sense view of religious problems, using whatever aid we can get from modern science and modern history. Now from that point of view there does not seem to be much importance in this discussion of the non-Christian references to Christ. We have to deal with them because the theme of this book is the historicity of Christ, and we have to ask whether, since there are no Christian witnesses except the late and anonymous Gospels and the Epistles of Paul, there are any Jewish or pagan witnesses. But for the reasons I have just given I should not be greatly astonished if there were none at all. What was Jesus, or the Jesus cult, to the Greeks and Romans of the first century? One Asiatic superstition amongst many. They would hardly hear of it. It was only when Christianity became an organized religion, giving trouble to the imperial authorities, that they could be expected to notice it.

The argument is less strong as regards the Jewish writers. The more learned of these, Philo, who was born about the same time as Jesus, could scarcely be expected to mention Jesus and his followers. He was an Alexandrian

Jew, and he wrote mainly on philosophy. An aristocrat of great wealth and culture, he would, even if he heard during his visit to Jerusalem of the new sect, not have any reason to speak of it in his works. His silence can mean no more than that Christianity was not of much importance in the world of his time.

It is very different with the historian Flavius Josephus. He was a Palestinian Jew, born at Jerusalem in 37 A.D., a man of high connections and great culture. He was intensely interested in religious questions, and he gives in one of his works so detailed an account of the Essenian monks with whom I shall suggest that Jesus was connected, that many suspect that he may for a time have lived in one of their monasteries. After the destruction of Jerusalem (70 A.D.) he resided in Rome and wrote his works, the chief of which are his *History of the Jewish War* and *Jewish Antiquities.* In one or other of these lengthy and exhaustive works he would, though a Pharisee, reasonably be expected to speak of Jesus and his followers. He even includes, in his *Jewish Antiquities,* a full and unflattering portrait of Pontius Pilate; and he tells of other zealots and reformers than Jesus in the Jewish history of the time.

Now in the *Jewish Antiquities,* as we have the book, we read the following pasage (xviii 3):

> About this time lived Jesus, a wise man, if indeed he should be called man. He wrought miracles, and was a teacher of those who gladly accept the truth, and had a large following among the Jews and pagans. He was the Christ. Although Pilate, at the complaint of the leaders of our people, condemned him to die on the cross, his earlier followers were faithful to him. For he appeared to them alive again on the third day, as godsent prophets had foretold this and a thousand other wonderful things of him. The people of the Christians, which is called after him, survives until the present day.

This passage is so obviously spurious that it is astonishing to find a single theologian left in our time who accepts it. No competent theologian or historian does. Josephus was a zealous Jew: and most of this is rank blasphemy from the Jewish point of view. There is a hint that Jesus was divine: he is said to have taught the truth, to have wrought miracles, and to have risen from the dead; and the messianic prophecies are expressly referred to him. To imagine Josephus writing such things is preposterous. It is a Christian interpolation.

But was a real reference to Jesus cut out by the Christian interpolator and replaced by this clumsy forgery? I have always held that that is probable, though some claim that the text of Josephus does not favor my idea. The passage about Jesus breaks in rather abruptly. Yet, clumsy as the forger was—making a zealous Jew recognize Jesus as "the Christ [Anointed One]" and the Messiah at the very height of the bitter feud of Jews and Christians—he would hardly pick any random page of the historian for his purpose. It seems to me not unlikely that he found there a reference to Jesus, and it would not be surprising if the last sentence of the passage, which would be just as clumsy for a later Christian to write, really is from the pen of Josephus.

It would seem that the new discovery *may* throw some light on this. Dr. Burch has certainly a singular way of publishing his discovery. It is going, he vaguely suggests, to help the faith materially; but it has first to help the sale of his book and the amount of his royalties, and incidentally the faithful will get consolation. I would hazard the opinion that there is nothing in it.

We are told that an ancient Slavonic version of Josephus' *Jewish War* (not the *Antiquities*) has been discovered, and that it contains testimony to the historicity of Christ. This may be one of two things. It may be a Christian interpolation in the *Jewish War* corresponding to the Interpolation in the *Antiquities:* or it may be a genuine Josephus reference to Jesus in sober terms. The former supposition is by far the more probable, since no later Christian would venture to cut out a reference to Jesus from our Greek version of Josephus (unless it was uncomplimentary).

Hence I think the Christian world, which is looking forward with palpitating heart to Dr. Burch's book, is doomed to one more disappointment. We must, in any case, leave open this question of Josphus. I do not gather that there has been any new discovery about the famous passage in *Antiquities*—and it is a palpable forgery. But there is reason to suspect that it was put in the place of a much milder reference to Jesus, and we therefore cannot impugn his historicity on the ground of "the complete silence of Josephus."

The next most important reference to Jesus is in the *Annals* of the great Roman historian Tacitus (xv, 44). He mentions the fire which burned down the poorer quarters of Rome in the year 64 A.D. It was suspected that Nero had ordered the fire, which caused great misery at the time, and, Tacitus says, the Emperor diverted suspicion by blaming the Christians for it and persecuting them. I will translate the entire passage from the Latin:

> In order to put an end to this rumor, therefore, Nero laid the blame on, and visited with severe punishment, those men, hateful for their crimes, whom the people called Christians. He, from whom the name was derived, Christus, was put to death by the Procurator Pontius Pilatus in the reign of Tiberius.

Tacitus goes on to describe how "an immense multitude" of Christians were put to death with fiendish torments, and were convicted "not so much of the crime of arson as of hatred of the human race."

This passage has many peculiar features. There cannot possibly have been "an immense multitude" of Christians at Rome in 64 A.D. There were not more than a few thousand two hundred years later. It sounds like a Christian interpolation. On the other hand, Tacitus has one of the most distinctive and difficult styles in Latin literature, and, if this whole passage is a forgery, it is a perfect imitation. We must, however, not press that argument too far. It is only the few words about the crucifixion that matter, and a good Latin scholar could easily achieve that. Professor Drews, indeed, who has a long and learned dissertation on the passage, believes it to be a forgery in its entirety, and argues that there was no persecution of Christians under Nero. He is not convincing, and it is difficult to believe—although there have been other scholars who agreed with Drews—that the passage generally was not written by Tacitus. The short sentence about Pilate may be an interpolation, but I know the peculiarities of the style of Tacitus too well to think the whole passage forged.

But why spend time over the matter? Tacitus is supposed to have written this about th year 117 A.D., or nearly eighty years after the death of Jesus. What does it prove? Only that after the year 100 there was a general belief in the Christian community that Jesus was crucified at the order of Pontius Pilate. That is nothing new. The reference to Pilate in I Timothy, whether Pauline or not, must be as old as that. Three of the Gospels were then written.

Some Christian writers argue that Tacitus must have seen the official record of the crucifixion. It is neither likely that any such official report would be sent to Rome nor that Tacitus looked up the archives, seventy years later, for such a thing. He was not the man to make such research or to be interested in such a point. If the passage is genuine, it shows only that there were in 177 A.D. Christians in Rome who said these things—which nobody doubts; and it is not certainly genuine.

I am inclined to accept it because another Roman historian of about the same date, Suetonius, has an obscure passage, in his *Life of Claudius* (Ch. xxvi), which seems to refer to the Christians: "Claudius expelled the Jews from Rome because, at the instigation of Chrestos, they were always making trouble." Chrestos was a not uncommon Greek name, and it is urged that it may have nothing to do with Christ. Claudius died in the year 54 A.D., and it is almost impossible to imagine that there was sufficient sectarian fighting between Jews and Christians at Rome over Christ—that is the only sense we can give to the sentence—before the year 54. On the other hand, the sentence would be quite meaningless as a Christian interpolation.

On the whole, since it would be two remarkable a coincidence to find the Jews rioting about a Greek named Chrestos when they were actually rioting about Christ, I prefer to think that Suetonius has heard, and has written in a confused way, about the Jewish reformer Christ. But it is of even less value than Tacitus. By the year 120 or 130 the cult of Christ was spread over the Roman world, and that is all that the mention by Suetonius implies.

Of Dr. Burch's twenty lines there remain only five in a letter of Pliny the younger to the Emperor Trajan. They say that the Christians were numerous enough in the province of Bithynia (Asia Minor), of which Pliny was Governor, to cause him concern. But he speaks of them as respectable, law-abiding folk who meet to sing hymns at day-break to Christ "as a God." A number of scholars have disputed the authenticity of the passage or the whole letter; and it hardly seems plausible that a Proconsul should write to the Emperor about such a matter. We need not, however, go into this. It follows only that by 113 there were a good many Christians in Asia Minor. Apologists merely reveal the desperate poverty of their case when they quote such things as these Latin sentences to prove that Jesus really lived nearly a century before.

We may conclude that no non-Christian writer of the

first century mentions Christ—Josephus being equivocal and certainly actually adulterated—and references in the second century are of no value at all. I repeat, however, that this need not impress us much. Josephus is the only writer who could reasonable be expected to mention Christ, and we do not know whether or not he did. The Christians remained a very obscure sect in a world that was seething with sects. That is all we can infer; and we knew it.

5

A Broad View

Many thousands of volumes have been written on the different aspects of this question, especially on the credibility of the gospel story. There is almost no part of my program which I find so difficult to compress into a Little Blue Book. Yet I think that I have given the reader the essential material for coming to a conclusion. Let us summarize it and see where we are.

The latin writers who are quoted as witnesses to the historicity of Jesus give us not the slightest assistance. They show, at the most, that Christianity existed in the second century, and that it was the common belief of the Christians that Jesus was crucified under Pontius Pilate.

Josephus is not a whit better. He may have mentioned Christ in his works, but we do not know. He certainly did not express a personal belief that Jesus was the Christ and Messiah, that he was probably superhuman, and that he rose from the dead; and therefore the actual passage in the *Antiquities* is spurious.

We are reduced to the testimony of Paul and the Gospels. Between 50 and 60 A.D. Paul repeatedly and emphatically asserts that he is in touch with men who knew Jesus personally and that Jesus lived in Judea and died on the cross. We have that assurance, and other details which we cannot exactly settle in an early Gospel, of about the same date or a little later, which is not lost. We then have the actual *Gospels* of our Bible; but they cannot be traced at all in the first century, and are therefore unreliable.

From this statement of the historical evidence we deduce at once that the customary fashion of making lives of Jesus out of the Gospels, or reading those Gospels as history, rests merely on an act of faith. Properly speaking, it is an expression of the will to believe, or a proof that the believer has never reflected on the bases of his belief. Any person is at liberty to believe that Christ walked on the water or rose from the dead. He is not at liberty to say that there is any serious historical evidence for those statements. It is absurd to count how many hundred people are said in the Gospels to have seen "the risen Lord." They are not witnesses. We have never heard them. An anonymous writer a hundred years after the event *says* that they saw the Lord, or thought or said that they did. One can say only, on Paul's authority, that the belief in the resurrection grew up very speedily after the death of Jesus.

Take any feature of the story of Jesus that you will. He likes to gather little children about him: he was gentle with adulterous women; he said that love was the greatest commandment; he lived in poverty and taught men ceaselessly. Your authority is always a biography which appeared, in its present form, nearly a century after his death. Not one single fact is known about Jesus from any source which we now have, written within half a century of his death, except what Paul says: that he taught and suffered and died in Judea about the time which tradition assigns to him.

In view of this late and quite unreliable character of the Gospel biographies I do not propose to analyze their contradictions and errors. It has been shown over and over again how they betray their lateness. For instance, the Pharisees are always represented as a comparatively small and exclusive set. On the contrary, they were in the time of Christ the overwhelming majority of the Jewish nation, of all classes. It is said that Christ taught in parables, and "not like the Scribes and Pharisees." That was precisely how the Pharisees taught. The writer is talking about an age he knows not.

There are predictions of the fall of Jerusalem which are plainly descriptions after the event of what actually happened in the year 70. There are twenty or thirty errors, counted long ago by Christian jurists, in the long description of the trial. There is a statement, much quoted by Catholics, that Jesus would found his "church" on Peter; and the word would have had no meaning at the time of Jesus. There are frequent references to tax-gatherers; and there were none in Galilee, except in Roman towns. Words in the language of Palestine are quoted and translated as if they are a foreign language to the readers.

Then there is the borrowed mythical element. The average believer would probably not give much for a Christianity without the picturesque birth in a stable and the resurrection. Both these are second-century stories; and both were certainly borrowed. Many less important statements are myths borrowed from the pagan religions. When we see how even the sentiments ascribed to Jesus are gathered from all quarters we shall realize even more plainly how our Gospels are compilations slowly increasing and gathering fresh material to the end of the first century.

It is a commonplace of religious literature that, if the Jesus of the Gospels did not exist, the creation of his personality by some obscure writers of the first century must itself be considered a miracle. Jesus is said to be "the grandest figure in all literature," and so on. The more the Modernist feels compelled to sacrifice the miracles and divinity of Jesus, the more zealous he is to magnify the grandeur of his personality.

Let us try, on the sober commonsense lines which we are following, to form an impartial opinion on this "figure of Jesus." Many Rationalist writers have used language about him just as superlative as that of the liberal theologians. Renan thought that there was "something divine" about Jesus. J. S. Mill was little less complimentary. Even Conybeare uses very high language. On the other hand, G. B. Shaw (in the preface to *Androcles*) bluntly says that Jesus was insane. George Moore (in the preface to his *Apostle*—one of the most refreshing impressions of the Gospels that you could read) says that the figure of Christ in *Luke*, to which the preachers generally turn, is "a lifeless, waxen figure, daintily curled, with tinted cheeks, uttering pretty commonplaces gathered from *The Treasury of the Lowly* as he goes by." A collection of the sayings about Jesus by able writers would beautifully illustrate the truth that on such subjects scarcely anybody tells the truth.

I have not the least interest in belittling the figure of Jesus. A liberal parson once genially asked me to "take off my hat to the universe." I replied that I was not a fool; but that I would not mind raising my hat to the figure of Christ on the cross—or of Bruno at the stake or Socrates in prison. But, mind you, these others met death more serenely than Jesus did: I mean, if we are to take Jesus as he is described in the Gospels. No amount of theological ingenuity will explain that "sweat of blood" in the garden of Gethsemane; and, if you point to the "Father, forgive them, for they know not what they do," I point to the other words, "My God, my God, why hast thou forsaken me?"

If you recall how Jesus loved little children, I remind you how by his advocacy of virginity as the higher ideal he cut at the root of family life and blighted lover, and how he believed in eternal torment for people of weak will. If you bring up the gentleness to the adulterous woman, I remind you of the bitter and rather vulgar abuse of the Pharisees, to which you will find no parallel in any pagan moralist of the time. In the Gospels Jesus utters hardly a single sentiment which, apart from chastity, he does not violate. He even scorns synagogues and meeting-places, and then founds a Church. He has not one word of guidance in the great problems of social life because he believes that the world is coming to an end. He is the archetype of the Puritans: scornful of all that is fair in life, bitter and unjust to those who differ from him, quite impracticable—nay foolish—in many of his counsels. It is absurd to say that our modern world has any use for Christ.

Now, the plain solution of all this tissue of contradictions, this mixture of sentiments of humanity with fierce intolerance, this gentleness to women and children and scorn of love and comfort, is quite easy after what we have seen: a dozen different conceptions of Jesus have been blended—or, not blended, mixed together—in these composite writings which we call the Gospels. Theologians have for ages perspired in attempting to reconcile the two different genealogies and other contradictions. It is waste of time. One man did not write any Gospel. One spirit did not dictate them. They emobdy the contradictory opinions of the isolated and often hostile communities in different parts of the Greco-Roman world. There is no "figure of Jesus" in the Gospels. There are a dozen figures. It was not the same man who made Jesus love children and scorn his mother. It was not the same man who made Jesus turn water into wine for marriage roisterers (probably singing what we now call indecent songs) and then advise us to live on bread and sleep on stones: who made Jesus the warm friend of the painted lady of Magdala and the advocate of barren isolation from all that is human. Jesus of Nazareth became in time the Jesus of Tarsus, of Ephesus, of Corinth, of Antioch, of Alexandria, and so on. The figure of the pale enthusiast was shaped and colored differently in a score of different environments. Paul's letters picture them for us. To one group he has to talk much about fornication and feasting, to another about correct ritual, to another about points of theology, and so on.

Must we, then, despair of finding any human Jesus

at all, and suppose that he is a myth who became man in the imaginations of his followers?

There are three chief reasons why I cannot agree with my learned friends in this. Let it be understood that there is no reason for bias either way. No Rationalist could in our time—whatever might be said of Matthew Arnold or Renan or Mill—be tempted to think that favoring the historicity of Jesus lessened the odium of his position. Most people now do not care a cent what you think about Jesus. A story circulates amongst the working men of Britain that a parson one day came with a parcel of tracts to a large group of workers, and asked one after the other: "My friend, do you know Christ?" One and all shook their heads, and at last one asked another why all this inquiry for "Christ." "Oh," said the other seriously, "there's a —— here brought him his dinner." That story is relished all over England. Middle-class and educated people are, as a majority, equally indifferent. And, as to the religious minority, if you deny *their* Christ, it does not matter the toss of a coin how much further you go.

But three things chiefly induce me, on a broad view of the whole subject, to think it probable that this reformer actually lived and was executed in Judea. The first consideration I give in the first chapter. It seems to me that the negative critics fail to give any serious evidence for their theory of a pre-Christian deity named Jesus.

Against these in particular, and against Couchoud and others who think Jesus a legend that grew up in neurotic minds, I feel the weight of the fact that the Jews themselves never questioned the historicity of Christ. Mr. R. T. Herford has carefully collected all the anonymous references to Jesus in the Talmud (*Christianity in Talmud and Midrash,* 1903). The Rabbis would not name the heretic, but they refer to him often. Instead of claiming that he was a mere myth, a deity turned into a man, the very earliest Rabbis treat him as an ordinary Galilean artisan, an illegitimate son.

The Jewish book which describes his father as a Greek or Roman officer is very late, and cannot be seriously quoted; but an early passage of the Talmud says that they have the genealogy of Jesus in the Temple, and that he was a love-child. A recent writer has suggested, and has much to say in support of his theory, that Mary was a maid in the service of the Temple; and maids in the service of temples have frequently become mothers. At all events, the Jews know nothing of a deity named Jesus or a myth. The Talmud was not committed to writing until a late date, but it is well known what precautions were taken to preserve the teaching of the important Rabbis of the first and second century. I say more about this when I show that most of the so-called parables of Jesus were actually taken from these Rabbis. The compiler of a Gospel, writing far away from Judea and decades after the event, who boasted that Jesus taught more simply than the Rabbis, was actually putting their teaching into the mouth of his own Master!

The third consideration is that, soberly using our common historical judgment, it seems far more probable that the phenomena of a Christianity in the first century imply an historical personage. I have not made a special study of the point, but from a general knowledge of Hindu and Chinese sacred literature I should say that we have less evidence of the personal existence of Kong-fu-tse or Buddha than of Jesus. The documents are even further removed from the events than the Epistles and Gospels are. Yet no historian doubts their historicity. Dr. Couchoud tells of a learned Buddhist priest who seems to have wondered how far Buddha was historical. But it is not clear fom his five or six words to Dr. Couchoud that he meant more than that actual details of Buddha's life were unreliable, as in the case of Jesus. The Persian prophet Zarathustra, whose personal existence has been seriously doubted, though the leading experts admit it, is in a quite different position. The documents are so late that the experts are not agreed within a few centuries about the date of Zarathustra. Apollonius of Tyana, again, is only known to us from a biography written more than a century after the events, yet no scholar has ever doubted his historicity.

Broad views are often the best views. We have a large number of historical and literary events to explain. Beyond any question there were great numbers of Christian churches in existence before the end of the first century. Probably Peter was never at Rome, but the other Roman bishops named, from about 70 A.D. onward, are not doubted. This group was a thousand miles from Judea; and there were churches all the way between, with over-seers (bishops), elders (priests), and servers (deacons). Lives of Jesus were circulating amongst them, and, with all respect to Professor Smith, those lives or Gospels do unquestionably represent Jesus as a man, living in Judea. The Church made short work of the Gnostics who held that Jesus was never contaminated by a bodily frame. Basilides, one of the ablest of the Gnostics, an Alexan-drian, tried to teach in the first half of the second century that Jesus was never a man; and the whole Church promptly and emphatically repudiated him. He had to found a special half-Persian, half-Christian sect.

The Epistles of Paul take us back to about the middle of the first century. There are then groups of Christians in every large city. They have no bishops or priests in the modern sense, but there are "elders" (*Timothy, Titus,* etc.), and there are some sort of higher men who appoint them and consider complaints about their conduct. It is clear that this situation existed certainly by 60 A.D. Paul was closer in touch with them all than any other man was. I am not relying on *Acts,* though part of it may be fairly early, but on the generally accepted Epistles. And Paul's gospel, which in these respects he does not find challenged anywhere, is quite clear. His belief in the phys-ical resurrection of Jesus is, he admits, not accepted by all. That belief is on a different plane. One could easily be mistaken about it. But that Jesus was born, taught, and was executed in Judea is at the very basis of Paul's teaching; and he never mentions any member of a church who doubts it. The Gnostics with their spiritual Jesus came later.

Moreover Paul, as we saw, habitually speaks of Cephas and others who were actual companions of Jesus. We have to deny the genuineness of all the Epistles to doubt this. In *II Corinthians* (iv 10) Paul says that it is fourteen years since he first came to believe in Jesus: that is to say, to believe that he was God, not that he was man. So he joined the Christian body, and mingled with them in Jerusalem, within less than ten years of the execution of Jesus. No Jew there seems to have told him that Jesus was a mere myth. In all the bitter strife of Jew and Christian the idea seems to have occurred to nobody. Setting aside the Gospels entirely, ignoring all that Latin writers are supposed to have said in the second century, we have a large and roughly organized body of Christians at a time when men were still alive who remembered events of the fourth decade of the century.

I conclude only that it is more reasonable to believe in the historicity of Jesus. There is no parallel in history to the sudden growth of a myth and its conversion into a human personage in one generation. Moreover, to these early Christians Jesus is not primarily a teacher. A collection of wise teachings might in time get a mythical name attached to it—though why the name "Jesus" it is hard to see—and the myth might in further time become a real person. But from the earliest moment that we catch sight of Christians in history the essence of their belief is that Jesus was an incarnation, in Judea, of the great God of the universe. The supreme emphasis is on the fact that he assumed a human form and shed human blood on a cross. So it seems to me far more reasonable, far more scientific, far more consonant with the facts of religious history which we know, to conclude that Jesus was a man who was gradually turned into a God.

6

Jesus an Historical Ghost

Jesus today is on the lips of the great majority of men only in profane expressions. The name of the Galilean peasant which held the world in thrall for fifteen centuries is now a swear-word, more frequently used by the vulgar than by the refined. I have seen the people of Greece and Serbia and Bulgaria, of Mexico and Spain and rural Italy, of the villages of Germany and Austria and Belgium and France, bowing with all the old awe at the utterance of the name. But they await only the coming of the teacher. They are overwhelmingly illiterate. Schools rise; and Christ sinks to a swear-word. One sees it happening in Serbia, Spain, Italy, and Mexico. By the end of this century the vast majority of men in Europe and America will be like the majority in any French, German, English, or American city: Christ-less.

So the majority of educated men are now no longer interested in any theorizing about Jesus. What does it matter whether or not there ever was such a person? A Papini, writing a new life of Christ with a misleading flavor of scholarship in it, finds quite a large circulation; but only amongst Christians, who are delighted to find that something apparently of intellectual distinction can still be

written on their side. Its utterly uncritical use of the Gospels and of legendary history makes the book unread-
able to ordinary men. And these men would now not take
the slightest interest in a critical study of Jesus. They
have done with him. He lived—let us see—about two thousand years ago. He said some pretty things in the Maeterlinck style, as George Moore says; but we prefer straight
practical talk about live problems. We can hardly realize
how Renan's *Life of Jesus* set the world on fire half a
century ago [1863].

Some would add that we not only do not want, but
won't have, Jesus in modern life. We no longer admire
crosses. We refuse to call sentiments "sublime" which no
reasonable person would think of acting upon. We are
better disposed toward Nietzsche, with all his paradoxes,
than toward Jesus. Only a few people ever did follow
Christ; and we have no room for them. There is a certain
logic, certain sound business, in mortifying your flesh and
remaining in an uncomfortable state called virginity, if
you are quite convinced that you thereby win a very superior sort of happiness for all eternity. Most Christians
seem never really to have believed it. Jesus certainly taught
it. All that is as out of date as the quill pen or velvet
trousers.

And it is just here that the question of Jesus does
retain a certain interest. A very large number of people
have not yet learned how to unite delicacy and refinement
of mind with frank sensuousness. They do not realize that
one gets more, not less, out of life by the combination.
As a result, we have still a large body of ascetics who
lean to the Jesus ideal. We are to live "the good life"—
why, we are not told—and save the world from sensual
demoralization. The world was never healthier; but these
people are not well acquainted with history. Men like
Belloc and Chesterton hear the cry, and they call out from
the door of the Roman tabernacle that *here* is the genuine
article. Fundamentalists and Modernists alike are zealous

to make profit by the supposed demand. The world still needs the Jesus ideal. The world is in danger of perishing for discarding it.

It would take many books to discuss this satisfactorily. When the world *did* accept Jesus, and as long as it was wholeheartedly Christian (in its convictions), it was piggish. The idea that believing in Jesus, either God or man, makes any race or generation refined and "spiritual" is a very naive ignoring of the whole of European history. What Jesus is supposed to have said—what every moralist was saying two thousand years ago—is of no use to us. Modern Chicago is slightly different from ancient Capharnaum. I was once compelled by circumstances to spend twelve hours walking about the streets of Adrianople, which is rather more advanced than a Galilean village. The idea of getting "guidance" from such a world was entertaining. But we will see later what there was of permanent human value in the "teachings of Jesus."

I cannot, in any case, conclude without some sort of historical suggestion about Jesus; and it happens that my conclusion really is of interest in connection with this modern question of whether or not we can dispense with him.

In an earlier chapter, I mentioned that Josephus, the chief Jewish historian, gives us so detailed an account of the Essenians of Palestine that he is believed by many to have joined them. We have already seen how this ascetic ideal appeared in the world long before Christian monasticism. It starts with a sheer superstition: but a superstition which many a philosopher has encouraged. Asceticism is supposed to promote "spirituality." I say that this is a superstition because the whole of literary history shows that sound thinking and good art may rather be expected from the man who is moderate with wine and love than from the man who knows neither. The ultimate or primary origin of the idea is, no doubt, the barbaric belief that the gods demanded sacrifices in their servants:

virginity in women, shaven polls or a fleshless diet or fasting, etc., in men.

At all events, there grew up in time a distinct creed that asceticism was the highest ideal of conduct. Buddha and others preached it in Asia, Zarathustra in Persia, Pythagoras and Plato and Zeno in Greece. It was fully developed in Egypt before the time of Christ. It breaks out in the rules for the priests and people in ancient Judea; and it steadily develops. The Pharisees thought fasts highly meritorious; and others thought the contamination of sex a thing to be avoided even more religiously than meat. The world has never yet recovered from its pre-historic shudder at woman's monthly disorder: which is really a clean and cleansing process.

As a result there developed in Judea, before the time of Christ, a monastic ideal cultivated by a body of men known as the Essenes or Essenians. Their origin is obscure. It seems to me that Persian influence on the Jews after the destruction of Babylon was the chief inspiration of it. The Persian ideal was, above all, one of purity. Buddhism, however, certainly reached Judea long before the time of Christ, and many think that it influenced in an ascetic direction both Jews and Greeks, and through them the Christians. What we do know is that in the time of Christ there were monasteries of these Essenian monks on the desert border of Palestine, and numbers of them living in the cities.

The Gospel writers never mention these monks; and I find that modern theologians do not like my bringing them to the notice of the modern world. But read this long description of their tenets and practices from Josephus (*Jewish War*, bk. II, ch. viii, paragraphs 2–14), as translated by Whiston:

> These Essenians reject pleasure as an evil, but esteem continence and the conquest over our passions to be virtue. They neglect wedlock. . . . They do not absolute-

ly deny the fitness of marriage and the succession of mankind thereby continued. . . . These men are despisers of riches, nor is there one to be found among them who hath more than another. . . . They have no one certain city, but many of them dwell in every city; and if any of their sect come from other places, what they have lies open for them, just as if it were their own. . . . For which reason they carry nothing at all with them when they travel into remote parts, though they have weapons with them for fear of thieves. [This is denied by Phillo, and is improbable.] . . . Nor do they allow of the change of garments or of shoes till they be first entirley torn to pieces, or worn out by time. Nor do they either buy or sell anything to one another, but everyone of them gives what he hath to him who wanteth it.

This is followed by a long account, which I need not quote, of their frugal meals, their frequent bathings (a Persian trait), and their daily labors and prayers. The historian continues:

Only these two things are done among them at everyone's free will, which are to assist those that want and to show mercy. . . . They are eminent for fidelity, and are the ministers of peace; whatsoever they say is firmer than an oath, but swearing is avoided by them, and they esteem it worse than perjury.

There is then an account of the procedure of initiation, two years' noviceship, baptism, two further years' trial, then formal admission. He concludes:

And before he is allowed to touch their common food, he is obliged to take tremendous oaths [vows]; that, in the first place, he will exercise piety towards God; and then that he will observe justice towards men; and that he will do no harm to anyone, either of his own accord or by the command of others; that he will always hate the wicked and assist the righteous; that he will ever show fidelity to all men, and especially to those in authority, because no one obtains the government without God's assistance; and that, if he be in authority, he will at no time whatever abuse his authority, nor endeavor to outshine his subjects, either in his garments or in any other finery: that he will be perpetually a lover of truth, and propose to himself to reprove those that tell lies: that he will keep his hands clear from theft, and his soul from unlawful gains.

Josephus here seems to me to confuse two bodies of men: some living in special communities or monasteries and others "in the world." A Roman Catholic would understand it on the analogy of the First Order (living in monasteries) and Third Order (married and other people in the world) of a modern monastic body. Philo expressly says that they lived in secluded monasteries: and, though this work is disputed, the Christian historian Eusebius tells us that a steward bought for them their garments and food out of a common fund. The Christian writer Hippolytus says (in his *Refutation of All Heresies,* IX, 18) that in their journeys "they possess neither two cloaks nor two pairs of shoes." They were perfect monks except in one respect: they were, Josephus says—and no other writer dissents— "the most virtuous men on earth."

Again I may ask the Christian who reads this description for the first time: What, in the name of common sense, could Jesus add to that? You have the quintessence of the teaching of Jesus in that summary of the teaching of the Essenes. Imagine one of these Essene monks going about Judea, as most of them evidently did. His conduct would be precisely that attributed to Jesus. Poverty, virginity, avoidance of oaths, passive resistance, aid to the unfortunate, love of all men, and so on. Then imagine one of their number of independent spirit, breaking with the main body. Imagine him obsessed with the idea that the Kingdom of God was at hand—that was a common Persian phrase for the end of the world and judgment of all men—and feeling that he was called to go and preach repentance, as the Essenes, apparently, did not. You have then, surely, something very close indeed to the Jesus of the Gospels.

It shows again how little the writers of the actual Gospels knew about Judea that they never mention these men, who were in every city. It is all "Scribes and Pharisees"; and even these are wrongly described. Jesus, for instance, is made to appear quite unique in telling men not to use oaths. Not only the Essenians, but the Pharisees, the great bulk of the Jewish nation, were enjoined to avoid oaths.

It seems to me, then, that the most reasonable historical view to take, in view of the scantiness of trustworthy evidence, is that Jesus, son of the carpenter Joseph of Nazareth (or some other village), joined the Essenes in his young manhood. They never married. They were recruited entirely from other families. From them he learned to abjure love and pleasure, to be content with one cloak, to have no settled residence, to despise the rich and never save anything, to heal the sick as well as he could, to share what he had with others. That is all pure Essenism.

But he was a young man of exceptional spirit. The Essenes simply declined to sacrifice. Jesus loathed the abomination, the whole sacerdotal system, and entered upon a campaign against it, getting a hearing in the synagogues. He was equally fiery against the rich. And, not being a mountebank and a money-maker like Billy Sunday, he drew crowds. Being a visionary, on the other hand, he thought that the end of the world was near, and he urged men to ignore what they called social life and polish their little souls for the day of judgment. I think it probable, too, that he came to think that he was a Son of God (in the Jewish sense), since some pretext for his execution for blasphemy is needed. And there seems to me to be too human a note in that "My God, my God, why hast thou forsaken me," to suppose that men who believed in his divinity fabricated and ascribed to him that cry of anguish. He was younger than Socrates, you see, and not a philosopher. And so he died on the cross, and they buried him in a rock-tomb, as they buried nearly everybody in that land of scanty soil. . . . A hundred years later, time for any conceivable legend to grow in the east, appeared the miracle-biographies of Jesus which we have.

That is what I conceive to have happened. Historically there is only the slenderest of evidence. Of his actual words it is not likely that anybody kept a record. He had not the slightest idea of founding a new religion, living in history, or influencing all men. He believed that the earth would be destroyed long before they could hear of him in Rome. The Gospels are compilations of Jewish and pagan moral sentiments of the time, harmonizing with the Essenian elements of the ideas of Jesus.

Bring the modern world back to that! The idea is childish. Few but priests, who would greatly profit thereby, can dream of such a thing. Goodbye, pale Galilean. It was not your fault that priests made a normal rule of life of the emergency-counsels of austerity which you gave in the belief that the end of the world was nigh. You are not responsible for the Middle Ages. They *used* you. It seems that, according to your poor light, you played a man's part. You denounced priests and priestcraft, and you told men to love one another. It is a pity, but not your fault in the circumstances, that you did not tell them to love women also. However, you were faithful to the end, by all accounts. You died for what you thought to be truth and the welfare of men. We think differently. Life is good and glorious. Love is the very flower of its sap. But we feel nearer to you than to the priests who affect to speak in your name.

Goodbye, dear Galilean.

How Christianity
"Triumphed"

1

The Legendary Triumph

The last sermon I ever heard, some fifteen years ago, was preached on board ship, in the middle of the Southern Ocean. From friendly clergymen I had heard of great reforms, audacious reforms, in the training of their preachers; and that evening the sermon was to be delivered by an Australian youth, just turned out, as a finished article, by a modern clerical manufactory. So I decided to hear the new gospel. He began with the pastoral story of Abraham. In five minutes he had reached the dividing by Moses of the waters of the Red Sea. In another five minutes he had come to the *labarum* of Constantine—he called it the *labahrum*—and I retired.

You may or may not know the story of the *labarum* which is said to have altered the course of history. Moses had divided the waters of the Red Sea; and the wicked nations had cheerfully pursued their wickedness. Jesus had divided the river of time into two parts, B.C. and A.D.; and the nations sinned and erred as gaily as ever. So, by a third *coup de main*, Jehovah put in the heavens something more convincing than a thunderbolt.

It was the year 312. All the blood of all the martyrs had converted only a small fraction of the Roman world, and a recent persecution had made apostates of ninety-nine in a hundred of those.

At that moment a fiery and unscrupulous, but very vigorous and ambitious man named Constantine, son of a rural barmaid who had dallied with a Roman officer, was leading a great army across Italy to meet his rival for the sovereignty of the world. Suddenly he saw, flaming on the heavens, the monogram (in Greek) of Christ, and, as if to prevent any nonsense about an ocular illusion, the words: "In this sign thou shalt conquer."

As is common in the case of these stupendous and unmistakable miracles, Constantine did not fall on his knees, but merely wondered. A second vision, during the night, informed him that his monogram referred to Christ; with whose religion and followers he had been familiar for ten years at least. After these two miracles he opined that Christianity was worth inquiring into. He inquired, was converted; and the real Christian Era opened. At Christ in a manger Greeks and Romans had mocked. By an emperor in the purple, with the police and soldiers behind him, their eyes were opened.

It is true that Christianity triumphed in the fourth century, and I devote three Little Blue Books to the explanation of the triumph. You will not learn *all* about it in these small pages, but you will learn a vast amount of essential historical truth and the evidence therefor. You may learn in another book that martyrs and miracles had nothing to do with it. The "Martyrology" is the largest compendium of lies every published. Christian teaching did not secure the triumph. What did?

First of all let us make quite sure that the triumph had not been substantially won, as orginary believers think, and religious writers encourage them to think, before the conversion of Constantine. How many Christians were there in the Roman Empire in the first decade of the fourth century? That means, remember, nearly three hundred years after the death of Jesus, two hundred and fifty years after the supposed "immense multitude" of Christians (fertilized by the blood of martyrs) at Rome, and two centuries after Pliny is believed to have said that the temples were deserted in Bithynia.

In so small a book you will hardly expect more than a quotation of the estimates given by the best authorities. I never give you less than that. But this point is of very great importance and interest, and we are going to study it for ourselves. One reason is that the estimate is difficult, and the figures vary from five millions to fifty millions! It is generally agreed that the population of the Roman Empire was at the time about one hundred millions, and I will set out here the estimates of the number of Christians among them that have been published by different historians who have made any sort of calculation:

Gibbon	5,000,000
Friedlander	5,000,000
Richter	6,000,000
Zockler	7,000,000
La Bastie	8,000,000
Chastel	8,000,000
Schultze	10,000,000
Keim	16,000,000
Matter	20,000,000
Staudlin	50,000,000

It must be difficult, mustn't it? As a matter of fact, it is not difficult to show that the larger estimates in this list, which are old and superficial guesses, are ludicrous, and even that the figure of five millions is too large.

Professor Bury, the most distinguished Roman historian in England and the very able editor of Gibbon's great work, generally agrees with Gibbon, but would put the figure higher at one time. As, however, he has made no personal study of the matter, I turn rather to the most recent and most scientific (or least unscientific) of all the estimates: that given by Professor V. Schultze, a Protestant scholar, in his *Geshichte des Untergangs des griechisch-römischen Heidentums* (2 vols, 1892).

Schultze makes a lengthy and detailed estimate of the number of Christians in each province of the Roman Empire; and, if you will take the trouble to tabulate the results (as he fails to do) and add them together, you will find a curious and significant thing. Apart from a few provinces where it is impossible to estimate the number of Christians, but where he admits that they were very few, his figures amount to 3,650,000. He would not ask us to add more than 100,000 for all the rest of the Roman world. Yet he concludes that there were "at least" 10,000,000 Christians in the Empire at the beginning of the fourth century, and he further says that Keim's figure, 16,000,000 is not too high! That is a nice sample of "religious statistics"; and Schultze was a distinguished professor and an expert.

But even the figure of 3,750,000 is too high. Having myself made a thorough study of the fourth century (see my *St. Augustine and His Age, Crises in the History of the Papacy, Empresses of Rome*, etc.), I can check Professor Schultze's deductions, and we shall find that he is too optimistic, even in his lower figure.

For most provinces of the Roman Empire he finds the number of bishops, and from this he estimates the number of the faithful. It is a delicate and treacherous method unless you know well the conditions of church-life in the fourth century. In my *St. Augustine* (pp. 195–7) I have shown that as late as the year 391, when Christianity was established by law and all other religions bloodily suppressed, the bishop of Hippo had only one church, with a few hundred worshipers, in a town of 30,000 inhabitants and that Augustine, who succeeded him had not a single priest under him; yet because Schultze finds 200 bishops in Africa about the year 310, he roundly estimates that there must have been 100,000 Christians. There is no known ratio of bishops and the faithful.

Next let us take Rome, where Schultze again finds 100,000 Christians (in a city of one million). We know that about the year 250, when the Church had enjoyed a long peace, Pope Cornelius had 46 priests, 14 deacons and subdeacons, 94 lesser clerics, and 1,500 widows and poor to support. From this Schultze and most other clerical writers (except Harnack) argue that there were 50,000 Christians in Rome in 250.

It would not be a monumental triumph, but in point of fact, I have shown from the official "Calendar of the Popes" that until the year 220 the Roman Christians had not a single chapel of any sort; and to imagine that they had chapels for 50,000 worshipers thirty years later is, in view of the stern law against them, absurd. As far as I can discover, they had only two.

Further we learn from the Christian historian Optatus that in the year 310, when Schultze estimates their number at 100,000, they had only forty small—very small—chapels. It would thus be more reasonable to suppose that at the outbreak of the Diocletian persecution they numbered about 20,000, and the persecution scattered them like chaff. Schultze's estimate of 100,000 Christians for the rest of Italy is even wilder. In the central and best educated part of the Roman Empire, Italy, which had a population of about 10,000,000, the Christians numbered certainly not more than 600,000 and probably much less. Schultze admits that in the next best educated provinces—Greece, Spain, and southern Gaul—they were very few in number.

The Christians were mainly in the ignorant east, especially Asia Minor (which had a larger population then than now) and Armenia. Antioch was the greatest city of the east, and it had half a million inhabitants. Its famous bishop and orator, St. John Chrysostom, tells us that he had in it 100,000 followers about the year 385. This was after *seventy years of imperial favor,* under the fanatically Christian Emperor Theodosius and the greatest orator of the Christian world. I would add that the figure is (as religious writers forget to say) a mere guess. What John really says, in a sermon in which he has every reason to exaggerate is: "I *believe* we reach the number of a hundred thousand." In any case, we can safely assume that seventy years earlier even at Antioch, the heart of eastern Christendom, there were not more than 50,000 Christians.

In short, it is liberal to grant, in the year 310, three million nominal Christians amongst the hundred millions of the Roman Empire; and the persecution had driven most of these back to the temples. Moreover, the vast majority were in rural Armenia (to which Schultze assigns no less than 2,000,000 out of his 3,75,000) Syria, and Asia Minor. The gospel, after nearly three centuries of propaganda, was a failure.

Hence we will not linger over the many pretty and ingenious theories of "the spiritual triumph" of Christianity, but the reader will expect a word about the five causes assigned by Gibbon in the famous fifteenth chapter of his *Decline and Fall:*

1. The inflexible zeal of the Christians.

2. The definite Christian doctrine of a future life.

3. The miracles claimed by the Church.

4. The pure and austere morals of the faithful.

5. The unity and discipline of the Christian Republic.

From other of this series, in which I prepare the reader for a proper conception of the rise of Christinaity, he may understand at once that Gibbon's speculations are due entirely to the imperfect condition of scholarship in his time. *The Decline and Fall of the Roman Empire* is not only the most elegantly written historical work that ever appeared, but it is for its age a model of conscientious industry and critical insight. Parsons who now jibe at its "errors" would do well to compare it with *clerical* works of the eighteenth century.

But our knowledge of the ancient world was at the time a mere legacy from the Middle Ages. Even Egyptologists had not begun their revelations; and Babylon— nay, even ancient Rome itself—still lay under the rubbish which a thousand years of semi-barbarism has heaped upon them. Nothing was known about "the pure and austere morals" of a half a dozen sects besides the Christian, or about the equally sure and certain hope of immortality which they offered to the pagan world. The vast library of lies and forgeries about the martyrs had as yet admitted only a few tremulous rays of truth; and Gibbon, in admiring the "inflexible zeal" of the Christians, was quite unaware that for every genuine martyr, voluntary or involuntary, a thousand Christians had offered incense to Zeus or bribed officials to certify that they had done so. The "miracles" were, we now see, not even known to the Christians themselves of the first three centuries. They are almost entirely the work of unscrupulous later ages.

This disposes of four of the fives causes; and the fifth cannot have been taken seriously by the historian himself. He would, of course, not know that there was just as much "discipline" amongst the Mithraists and Manichaeans, the worshipers of Isis, and the devotees of the Greek mysteries. But he did know that instead of being "one," the Church was bloodily rent by schisms and heresies; that, instad of being a republic, its constitution was intensely autocratic by the third century; and that what it had of unity and discipline was precisely what annoyed the Romans and moved good Emperors to persecute it.

We understand Gibbon, but we can make only the excuse of culpable ignorance for religious writers who in our time find "causes" of the miraculous spread of Christianity. One of the most popular and most mendacious of these is the claim that it was unique in welcoming the slave and the woman on equal terms. This was done by the Mithraists, the Manichees, the Stoics, and the religious trade-organizations (or Colleges). And it is equally untrue that the Christian body attracted by its virtues—the sermons of the Fathers are one long indictment of its vices—or would be likely to attract the ignorant masses of the Roman world, who formed the great bulk of its adherents, by such an expensive advertisement.

There is no miracle or marvel to be explained. In three centuries the new religion may have won three million followers. The old Roman, Greek, and Asiatic religions were in decay, discredited by their own thinkers. It was the easiest thing in the world to ridicule the old polytheism. A very large number of people were ready for alternatives. From St. Augustine we gather that the Manichaeans were at least as numerous as the Christians. Modern experts on Mithraism say that it was even more prosperous. It was adopted by emperors before Christianity was. A period of evolution had been reached when new religions were bound to spread, and historical parallels are abundant. One instance will suffice: In the nineteenth century Spiritualims won three million people (out of four millions) in the United States in ten years, whereas it took Christianity nearly three centuries to reach that number in a world of gross ignorance and superstition. The spread of the Albigensian heresy in the Middle Ages was even more rapid and complete.

The growth was chiefly in the third century, and there was a special reason for this. Incessant war had very greatly impoverished the Empire, and the Christians of the cities, where they had a few rich adherents, made charity a very important part of their work. The church at Rome supported 1,500 widows and indigent in the middle of the third century. The Church at Antioch maintained 3,000 in the fourth century. The Romans were accustomed to parasitism by their own vicious system (see Little Blue Book No. 1078), and they appreciated this gospel of charity.

On the whole, however, there was no growth that is historically unusual or puzzling. That is the main point. Friedlander, who was one of the most thoroughly informed writers on Rome, though his study of this point is slight, says that, before Constantine, the Church won one-twentieth of the Empire. Schultze, who has made the least superficial estimate, says one-tenth; but his *figures* amount to less than one-twentieth. The only problem is: How was the 4 or 5 percent converted into 100 percent?

2

The "Conversion" of Constantine

Let us return for a moment to the dear old *labarum:* one of the most profitable miracles that the hand of God, or of his earthly representative, ever achieved.

It is Eusebius, the bishop of Caesarea, who tells us of the miracle in his *Life of Constantine;* and you ought not to doubt it for a moment, because he says that he heard it from the Emperor's own lips! We will not, however, waste time in psycho-analytic research. I do not think that any ecclesiastical historian today believes in the vision, or even suggests an ocular illusion. All other historians smile at it. The *labarum* is as discredited as Catherine's wheel.

"The father of ecclesiastical history," as Eusebius of Caesarea is unhappily called, wrote his famous Ecclesiastical History some years before the death of Constantine; and it does not contain this very important miracle. When the Emperor died, however, the bishop wrote a most untruthful and eulogistic *Life of Constantine,* and in this he tells the story of the *labarum.* He tells us also that his chief business as a writer is to "edify"; which means, to advertise the Church. So modern historians are discreetly reticent about the zealous and courtly bishop. I will, as usual, supply the word which they leave unspoken. Eusebius was a liar. The other great Christian writer of the time, Lactantius, is by no means a model of veracity. But he merely says that Constantine saw the vision in a dream. The *labarum* appears on coins soon after the conversion of Constantine, but no one pretends that it was a reality except Eusebius.

This conversion of Constantine is one of the unsolved, or imperfectly solved, problems of history. Thousands have written on this event, which certainly changed the history of the world, yet there is no agreement whatever. The Emperor was not baptized until the shadow of death fell upon his path. Years after his supposed conversion he used language ("The divinity in the heavens above") which any educated pagan would use. No one knows his real beliefs; any more than we know the beliefs of Napoleon. But we will not attempt here to discover them. He *adopted* Christianity, and that was the beginning of its triumph.

Constantine was, as I say, the illegitimate son of a rural barmaid and a Roman officer. The educated Romans always hated and despised him, and they do not conceal his birth. St. Ambrose, in fact, tells it. His father Constantius was an officer of distinction in the Roman army, and a robust tavern-wench, afterwards dignified with the name of Helena, in an outlying rural province of the Empire, caught his soldierly fancy. She was so fortunate as to become the mistress of one who was destined for the purple; and, as if Providence did not deem that enough, her purblind generosity to the clergy earned in time for the Bithynian barmaid—a profession next door to that of courtesan—the chaster halo of the saint.

In Constantine the blood of the peasant-girl counted for more than that of Constantine the Bloodless (as his name means), and the aged Emperor Diocletian regarded him with some anxiety. But the political circumstances here throw more light than miracles do on the course of events, and I will explain them as briefly as possible.

When that fine old Roman, Diocletian, had reorganized and pacified the Empire he chose a colleague, Maximian Hercules, to assist him in ruling it, and he raised to the rank of Caesars (princes with some hope of succession) Galerius and Constantius. Galerius was a somber and zealous adherent of the old religion, and it is said that it was he who egged Diocletian on to persecution of the Christians; though Diocletian never urged the death-sentence for religion, in spite of revolt and insolence and even arson in his own palace.

Constantius, on the contrary, seems to have been an easy-going and more or less cultivated man. He believed, with the Greek and Roman philosophers, in one god whose reality was figured or caricatured in all the deities of the Roman religion; and there can be little doubt—indeed, it is clear—that he transmitted his mild philosophy to his son Constantine. But Diocletian sent Constantius to rule Gaul and Britain, and kept the son in the east. When in 303, Diocletian began to persecute, Constantius evaded the application of the decrees in his provinces. There were few Christians in them, and he would see no menace what-ever in their peculiar beliefs and practices. His leniency became known thoughout the Church, and the Emperor Galerius suspected that there was a political aim in his protection of the Christians. Diocletian and his colleague had abdicated in 304, and Galerius, now promoted to be emperor in the east, with Constantius as emperor in the west, prevented the young Constantine from obtaining the rank of Caesar.

I will not drag the reader through the details of the bloody civil wars that followed upon this multiplication of ambitions, but the question of sparing or favoring the Christians of the Empire now became, to use modern lan-guage, a plank in the political platform. Religious writers affect to see in this a confirmation of their very large figures of the number of Christians. It proves nothing of

the kind. In a contest which seems fairly even and uncertain the support of any fanatical minority is useful.
Moreover, there was the air of political wisdom which
a man might have in proposing to put an end to religious
dissensions in the hard-pressed Empire. It would appeal
to educated pagans.

Constantine escaped and joined his father in Britain;
and very shortly afterwards the father died, and his troops
acclaimed Constantine Emperor. Ferrers, the latest student
of the period, believes that the young Constantine engi-
neered this *coups,* and it is the kind of thing he would
do. Galerius, however, refused to recognize the election,
and he made Constantine a Caesar. There was then a series
of civil wars with which I need not complicate this sketch.
In 310 Constantine beat and strangled the old Emperor
Maximian, whose daughter Fausta he had married; and
in 312 (the *labarum* year) he set out for Rome to try his
strength against his brother-in-law Maxentius.

This complicated quarrel put an end to the persecution.
Galerius had died of cancer in 311, but some months before
he died he withdrew his persecuting decrees and addressed
the Christians in quite amiable terms. We are told, of
course, that as a last resort he was turning to Christ to
heal his cancer. Moreover the Emperor Maxentius in Italy,
against whom Constantine was advancing, also thought
it prudent to disarm the Christians who were likely to
do anything in their power to aid Constantine. He granted
full liberty of conscience. These were the circumstances
when, in 312, Constantine led his legions into Italy and
was "converted" on the march. Maxentius was beaten.
Constantine, now Emperor, met his co-Emperor Licinius
at Milan and together they issued a formal Edict recog-
nizing the freedom of the Christians.

This famous Edict of Milan was not, as is commonly
said, the first chapter of liberty. The Christians were already free, except that the Emperor Maximian still persecuted in the east; though he in turn was killed in 313.

Constantine, in the next year, attacked and beat Licinius, but he continued to share the empire with him for nine years, when, at the close of a fresh struggle, he had him treacherously murdered. Let me add here that three years later again, in 326, Constantine had his wife Fausta, his illegitimate son Crispus, and his nephew, murdered in his palace at Rome. Clerical writers try in vain to shift from him the guilt of these new crimes. The evidence is overwhelming. It is clear that the illegitimate son of the illegitimate Constantine was guilty of some outrage in regard to his beautiful and refined step-mother, and in a blaze of temper Constantine ended their lives.

It is in the light of these events that we have to judge, if we wish to do so, the character and "conversion" of Constantine. He remained the head—Pontifex Maximus, or Sovereign Pontiff—of the old Roman religion until he died. He in 321 ordered the *auspices* (or religious diviners) of the pagan religion, against whom he had issued a severe decree, to make their exploration of the entrails of birds as usual if the palace were struck by lightning. In the following year he instituted the Sarmatian Games, with the usual religious (pagan) accompaniments, to the scandal of the Christians. In 330 he ordered the closing of two of the gayest temples of Aphrodite in the east; and they were either not closed or were reopened at once. Some of his coins represent him in the robe of the Pontifex Maximus, and pagan orators addressed him as if he were one of themselves. He, in fine, deferred his baptism (by water—he was amply baptized in blood) until the approach of death recommended to him this easy method of obliterating his crimes; and after death the pagans elevated him, as was customary, to the rank of a divinity.

On the other hand—and this is all that concerns us— he established the principle of persecution of the old religion, and his massive generosity to the Chruch lifted it in twenty years to a position of which it had never dreamed. Was he a Christian? Was he, as the pagan historian Zosimus says, an adherent of the old religion (in his father's way) until the scorn of Rome for the murder of his wife and son drove him entirely into the arms of Christians? Or was it, until the end, merely a policy of creating a very powerful organization, intensely attached to himself, out of the Christian body? I choose the last alternative.

But it remains to tell what he did for the Church, for this is the real foundation of the triumph of Christianity. By the beginning of the year 311 the Church must have been smaller and more depressed than it had been since the first century. The few hundred who were prepared to die for the faith had been martyred. The great majority had concealed whatever faith they had under a profession of paganism. It was mainly in the rural districts of the east that any large number still clung to the religion of Jesus.

Constantine probably overestimated the number of Christians in Rome, Africa, and the East. He had lived six years in Britain and Gaul, and he knew the extent of the sect only from the exaggerated language of the pagans themselves. We must constantly bear in mind that in those days there were no statistics. Long afterwards, as I have said, St. John Chrysostom had no accurate knowledge of the number of the faithful in his own "parish," which was the best organized in Christtendom. Every writer of ancient times who speaks about the number of the Christians merely gives us an impression of little or no value.

Upon this scattered and dejected Christian world of the year 311 there then came, in succession, the news that Galerius had suppressed persecution and was dying of cancer; that Constantine, whom rumor regarded as a patron and deliverer, was on his way to Rome to seize the throne; and.that Maxentius, the actual ruler of Italy and Africa, had been forced to grant them full liberty. Certificates of pagan orthodoxy were cheerfully burned, and the faithful returned to the foot of the crucifix. Next year came the news of Constantine's victory at the Milvian Bridge; and in 313 the formal charter of liberty was signed by Constantine and Licinius at Milan. But Constantine immediately went beyond this declaration of religious neutrality and evinced an attitude of what is now called benevolent neutrality. In the same year, 313, he exempted the Christian clergy from municipal offices. In the Roman administration these local functions, so far from being paid, were extremely costly and onerous to the citizens who were compelled to discharge them, and there was a very general attempt to evade them. Exemption was regarded as so valuable a privilege that the Christian clergy now discovered a remarkable number of "vocations" to their body, and great disorder ensued in the municipal administration. I leave it to the Catholic historian Count Beugnot (*Histoire de la destruction du paganisme*, I, 78) to estimate the result:

> The effect of this measure was soon felt. On all sides one saw crowds of people make for the churches who were moved not so much by conviction as by the hope of reward; and this first favor granted to Christianity admitted to its bosom guilty passions which had hitherto been foreign to it, passions which had speedy and pernicious consequences. The complaints of the municipal bodies and the disorder that followed in the administration of the provinces soon compelled Constantine to modify the privilege.

This, in fact, was Constantine's invariable experience when he listened to clerical suggestions of legislation in their favor. The anger of his solidly pagan Empire compelled him to withdraw. In 319 he issued a savage decree that any *auspex* who entered the house of a citizen should be burned alive, though the *auspices* might continue to function in the temples. It is said that the aim of the decree was to prevent the fraudulent exploitation of the citizens by private fortune-telling for money, but, as Beugnot observes, the real aim was a deadly blow at the old religion by making impossible the assumption of its offices. Two years later Constantine was forced to modify, or virtually repeal, his law, and it was probably never applied.

In the same year, however, he tried to impose the Christian Sunday as a day of rest on his Empire. How stupid or ignorant is the idea that the Christian Church brought a great boon to the Roman worker with its one day's rest out of seven. The Romans rested on the Thursday (Thor's or Jupiter's Day—*Dies Jovis*), and, as I said, they had more than a hundred holidays in addition in the year. Constantine's aim was, as in his previous measures, to enforce Christianity. Again, however, he failed, and he had to modify his own decree.

Then came the dreadful year 326, when he, in the very heart of the Empire, murdered his son and daughter. In my *Empresses of Rome* (1911) I have carefully analyzed all the original authorities in regard to the character of Helena, the illegitimacy of Constantine (which Gibbon chivalrously denied), and these murders. Constantius *could not* validly marry Helena in Roman law. As to the murders—of a son, wife, and a young nephew—the evidence is so clear that no one but a Roman Catholic historian now doubts it. There is further evidence of a respectable kind that Fausta was barren, that the three sons of Constantine were born of his mistress Minervina, and that she also was murdered at some time. Anyone who cares to consult my book, which is throughout based upon the Latin and Greek writers of the time, will see that the pagan empresses, up to the end of the fourth century, were as a rule reputable women; and that with the conversion of imperial ladies to the new religion we enter upon a story of intrigue, passion, and vindictiveness which if far more picturesque. The contrast is even more marked in my *Empresses of Constantinople*.

The Greek historian Zosimus tells us that after the murders at Rome the Emperor applied for purification in the temple of Jupiter, and, the pagan priests sternly refusing, he turned to the Christian priests, who consented. This is fable, but it embodies fact. Rome, which was still overwhelmingly pagan, drove out the Emperor with its scorn and indignation. He was a barbarian. Christianity received him, at least more intimately than before. He went to Asia Minor, and there he converted the old town of Byzantium into a new capital of the Empire, Constantinople. H. G. Wells, whose treatment of the pagan nations is deplorable, expatiates on the profound strategical wisdom of forming a second capital in the east. It is true that the plan had been decided, and the work begun, before 326. But the chief motive was the scornful opposition of Italy to his religious designs and the determination to create a new and wholly Christian Empire. When Constantine found pasted on the gate of his Roman palace an inscription which I may translate,

> Say ye the Golden Age of Saturn dawns again?
> Of Nero's bloody hue these jewels are,

he fled. Fausta was a very beautiful and, as Julian himself tells us, most refined and virtuous lady, and she was only thirty-four or thirty-five yearss old at the time when her husband murdered her. It is clear from the historians that Helena, his Christian mother, stung him into committing the murder; and it is highly probable that Fausta had justly accused his son and so incurred the fierce anger of Helena.

From the first Constantine had, apart from his unsuccessful decrees, showered wealth and privileges upon the Church. A stream of gold flowed from the palace, and new churches, of a more attractive nature, began to rise. At court and in the army the best way, if not the only way, to secure promotion was to become convinced by the brilliant evidence of the religion. Even ordinary citizens were rewarded with a baptismal robe and a piece of gold. Villages were raised to the rank of cities if all their inhabitants exchanged Jupiter for Christ. In ten years imperial gold had done more than the blood of all the martyrs, the miracles of all the saints, and the arguments of all the apologists.

Except that wealth continued to reach the Roman clergy, the progress of the Church in the est was now suspended. The city of Constantinople was dedicated in 330. The world had at least a Christian metropolis; and it was a superb city. Already, as I said in the first chapter, more than three fourths of the Christians were in the ignorant east, and they were now encouraged to attack pagan temples and openly ventilate their scorn. Few pagans could get advancement in the east. Constantine had lost all his vigor and clear wit. Dressed in effeminate robes, laden with jewels, crowned by a mass of false hair, he sat amongst the women and priests who now "converted" the world by means of his money and favors. Only now and again did the old anger burst, when the quarrels which rent the Church, from Africa to Mesopotamia, showed him how futile was his dream of a spiritual empire or, as Napoleon would later say, a spiritual gendarmerie. But he had chosen; and he had opened a new chapter of the human chronicle. He was baptized, and died, in 337.

3

The Martyr Turns Persecutor

I have said that Constantine, who seems never to have been a convinced Christian—though we would gladly make the Church a present of him—established the principle of persecution. His attempts to destroy or enfeeble the Roman religion by his savage legislation against the *auspices,* and to supplant Jupiter's Day by the Christian Sunday, justify this statement. He was, however, defeated; he was forced by his people reluctantly to observe his benevolent neutrality.

His Christian panegyrists boast that he "closed the temples." Beugnot finds only an order to close three temples, two of which were *not* closed, but in the east his favor no doubt encouraged the Christians to destroy a few temples in villages where they had the majority. His work for the Church—and it was monumental—was to endow it with prodigious wealth and bribe men by promotion to embrace it. By his prodigal generosity to the Church and the building of his Christian capital he farther enfeebled the Empire and accelerated its fall.

An ever graver blunder was that he had, without naming a successor to the throne, divided the rule of the Empire between his three sons, two nephews, and other relatives. These and their Christian supporters now crowded into the Christian palace at Constantinople, and it was soon reddened by a crime as sordid and ghastly as any that Nero had ever committed. Since moreover, historians are generally agreed that the author of it was the man who was now to realize the aspiration of the clergy, and attempt the bloody suppression of all religions except the Christian, it deserves our consideration.

Constantine's three sons, said to be illegitimate sons, Constantine (aged twenty-one), Constantius (aged twenty), and Constans (aged seventeen) had been trained by the clergy and were fanatically Christian. Constantius, the modern Christian may eagerly say, had embraced the Arian (or Unitarian) heresy; and I willingly concede it. He was the most profoundly religious of the three, the most resolute in persecuting paganism, the most priest-ridden, and the only one of the three who embraced Christianity in its least unintellectual form, Arianism. Eusebius of Caesarea, who had baptized and now came to burn Constantine, also was an Arian. And I stress this because it is an Arian historian, Philostorgius, who tells us the story of what happened. He would not libel and Arian emperor and an Arian bishop.

Constantine, he says, left a will in which he accused his two step-brothers of having poisoned him. Insofar as there were "heirs to the throne" in the Roman Empire, these men were the heirs. The will had been given to Bishop Eusebius, but Eusebius, anxious not to be too closely connected with it, put it in the hands of the dead emperor and let them discover it there. The statement in it was made known to the troops, and they murdered the two step-brothers, seven nephews, and several cousins of the dead emperor, with a number of distinguished courtiers. The empire was then divided between the three sons.

It is a sufficient reflection on the regime of virtue and magnanimity inaugurated by the new religion that from the year 310 onward the path of the historian is strewn with problems. Murders and outrages occur every few years—I have not mentioned all—and a signficant obscurity envelops them all. But we have, here again, so much evidence that few historians now hesitate. The most religious of the three brothers, Constantius, was the leader of this polot. The best that is said for him is that the plot was proposed to him by the officers and merely endorsed by him. The forged will was part of the plot; and one would very much like to know what was the real relation of Bishop Eusebius to it. In any case, no one now doubts the guilt of Constantius. His father had waded through blood to the throne. The son secured it by at least sanctioning an orgy of murder.

Fortunately, one boy escaped the massacre, and he lived to become the Emperor Julian. "Julian the Apostate," the modern Catholic scornfully calls him; and he then bows to the memory of "Constantine the Great" and his bloody sons. How long, O Lord, before thou dost deliver thy people—from priests?

Constantine, the eldest son, soon joined the shades of the dead. Within three years he was fighting his brother and, under suspicion of murder, he disappeared. Gallus, a nephew who had, like Julian, been saved from the massacred, was murdered later. Julian grew up in terror and daily danger of murder. Constans, the youngest emperor, an orthodox Christian, proved another Elagabalus. He so openly paraded the handsome peasant youths with whom he committed unnatural vice that his general rebelled, and he was murdered. I need only say of him that until his death, in 350, he piously joined his brother Constantius in issuing the sanguinary decrees which were to force the Empire to embrace the gentle and ascetic teaching of Jesus.

Religious readers, in whose literature these things are never mentioned—indeed, few of their writers or preachers know anything about the time, the most critical phase in the history of their religion—will suspect that I am reproducing the strained inferences of "advanced" or "extreme" students of history. Those who have read other books of mine will know that I never do anything of the kind. In fact, I am as familiar with the original Greek and Latin authorities as any historian, and I am quoting nobody. I may add that there is nobody who doubts that Fausta, Crispus, and Licenius were murdered in 326, that Constantine's two step-brothers, seven nephews, and many others were murdered in 337, and that Gallus and Constans were murdered later; and the great majority of the modern authorities assign the guilt as I have done.

This Emperor Constantius, then, was the second great instrument of Providence in securing the triumph of Christianity; and he did far more than his father. Let me, however, finish with the other members of this first Christian royal family and concentrate on the emperor. Of Constantine's sisters one, Anastasia, saw her husband murdered in the massacre and soon followed him; the other, Eutropia, was murdered with her son by an adventurer patronized by her niece Constantina. This daughter of the later emperor, whose husband had been included in the massacre, at length married the youthful Gallus, who had been saved from it, and the royal pair illumined the city of Antioch with a license of morals that would have made the old priestesses of Aphrodite blush, and with a ferocity of temper that betrayed their barbaric blood. They were lured to Italy, to be murdered, by Constantius; but Constantina died on the way and left Gallus alone to receive the knife. It seems clear that Julian was destined for the same fate, but the brilliant and blameless youth won the affection of the empress and was protected by her, as we shall see.

This imperial adept in murder, whose grandmother had served wine to soldiers in a wayside inn of the lower type, was from the first urged by Christian writers to give effect to his profound and very real piety by persecuting the pagans. Firmicus Maternus, one of the leading

Christian scholars of the time, laid at the feet of the emperor his work *On the Errors of the Profane Religions* and implored him to end them. "With a little further effort," he cried, "the devil will be prone, slain by your laws, and the baleful pest of idolatry will perish." "Tear away, tear away without fear, most sacred [!] emperors, the ornaments of the temples," he shrieks again. It was only a few years since Christian writers had written eloquently about the right of every man to cherish his own religion.

But doubtless Eusebius of Caeserea was the "chief inspirer," if so pious a man as Constantius needs inspiration. Less than four years after the death of Constantine his two sons—the murderer and the sodomite—issued a formal decree forbidding the exercise of the pagan religion under sentence of death. I translate the text of this edict of the year 341 from the Latin in Schultze's useful work:

> Let superstition cease. Let there be an end of this insanity of sacrificies. Whoever, in opposition to the law of our *divine* parent and prince and this command of our *clemency,* shall dare to offer sacrifice shall be visited with condign punishment and speedy sentence. (Law in the Theodosian Code.)

Schultze says that we learn from Libanius that the sentence, which is not specified, was death; and he justly observes that the ascription of such a law to Constantine is a lie and a trick. One may safely attribute it to Bishop Eusebius.

The magistrates of the Roman world seem to have ignored this savage edict, and shortly afterwards there appeared another, which again I will translate literally from the Latin:

> It is our pleasure that the temples be closed at once in all localities and towns: that access to them be forbidden to all and thus the opportunity of transgress-

ing be removed from wicked men. We require also that no one shall offer sacrifice. And if any do perpetrate anything of this kind, let him perish by the sword of vengeance. (Law in the Theodosian Code.)

Such things were issued by the Christian Emperors at a time when Christian writers had hardly ceased to complain of the diabolical inspiration and utter immorality of the late persecutions. And not a single Christian leader of the time protested. St. Athanasius, who had seen the Diocletian horrors and had in turn felt the pressure of Arian persecution—Constantine had in the end banished *him* for his irrepressible turbulence—did not open his mouth. The moral tone of the Christian body was low, as we have already seen and will see more clearly, and the cry of "vengeance" was passing from lip to lip.

A few years later the religious policy was again modified by the political circumstances. Magnentius, the adventurer whom Constantine's virago of a daughter had patronized, assumed the purple in Gaul, the Emperor Constans wa slain, and the usurper, though a Christian, played for pagan support by granting fully liberty of worship. Constantius went west and defeated him, and the law against the old religion was repeated:

Let all nocturnal sacrifices, which Magnentius had permitted, cease at once, and let the abominable permission be henceforth refused.

In fine, in 356 the death-sentence was renewed:

We command that sentence of death be passed on any who are convicted of offering sacrifice or worshipping idols.

These laws, not the sacrifices of the martyrs or any miracles of supernatural power, inaugurated the triumph of Christianity in the east. In the west—in Rome, Italy, and Roman Africa—they were probably not enforced. In fact, Constantius himself visited Rome in the year 357, and the sight of its solid paganism converted the lion, for the duration of his visit, into a lamb. He confirmed the privileges of the Vestal Virgins and the priests. He permitted sacrifices. He conducted himself with perfect urbanity when his pagan hosts took him to inspect the famous temples of the city. The "games," which always opened with a religious service and procession, were untouched, for Christians as well as pagans, both in east and west, clung to the bloody spectacles of the amphitheater.

Historians dispute how far the edicts of Constantius were carried into effect in the east. I have said that in the more ignorant parts of the east Christians were already, at the beginning of the century, three or four times more numerous than they were in the west, and the removal of the court to Constantinople watered these Christian nurseries with a stream of gold. However, words of St. John Chrysostom which I have already quoted warn us not to exaggerate. Christian writers of the time of Constantius exult in the dying of paganism and loudly proclaim that almost the whole world is Christian. Yet even in 385 Chrysostom can only boast that he *believes* that one fifth of the population of Antioch is Christian. In the country, possibly, the propaganda would have more success, though it was the opposite in Italy.

We have no record of any pagan being put to death under the new laws, though many were executed for "divination" and some of these may really have been pagan martyrs, but it is clear that temples were generally closed and were destroyed in many places. Wherever a local fanatic could count upon a sufficiently large crowd of followers, the axe and the torch were set in motion. Constantius appropriated the revenues of the temples, many of which had ample property, and with these funds he bought new converts to the faith. Sycophants, spies, and hypocrites swarmed about him. In one decree he enacted that all the non-Christian temples should be destroyed, and the sites and material given to the Christians to build churches. At other times he gave the temples to his converts or favorites, and they were used as stables or mansions. It is on record that in one instance Constantius allotted a beautiful and revered pagan temple to the whores of the two as their residence and place of business.

The result was a disorder and acrimony which further enfeebled the sinking empire and an enlargement of the Church at the cost of whatever character it possessed. Christians like Constantius, Constans, Gallus, and Constantina permitted the pagans to think that the Church would not really insist on the austere code of morals which its founder had recommended. Men and women of weaker character or more cynical standards of life changed their religion to the new pattern. Men pointed them out in the streets of Constantinople and Antioch as men who had become rich on the spoils of the temples.

Others joined the new religion in the belief that its power was only temporary, and that the thunder of Jupiter would yet punish the tyrants and profaners of temples. The Emperor Julian tells us that when he visited the site of Ilion in 354 the local bishop confided to him that he was an adherent of the old religion, and prayed in secret to Helios, but he had joined the Church in order to be able to protect the temple until the day of restoration. In other places, Athanasius tells us, Arians joined with pagans in wreaking vengeance on the orthodox Christians and befouling their churches as only Asiatics can. To desecrate the consecrated host of a rival chapel with one's excrements became a Christian pastime. "He is building churches—and destroying the faith," said St. Hilary of Poitiers scornfully of the Emperor.

The pagans began to look to Julian for a restoration. It is absurd, in view of the previous murders, to affect to believe that Julian was not in constant danger of death. Constantius had no heir; and writers of the time hint that his one undeniable virtue, chastity, had a secure foundation in his own morbid constitution. His court was full of corrupt eunuchs, one of whom was so powerful that the Roman writer Ammianus Marcellinus remarked that the emperor seemed to have a certain influence with his chief eunuch. Bishops were the next in influence, and we have more than one record of their growing arrogance.

Julian buried himself in study to divert suspicion— a choice which soon taught him to loathe the religion he was compelled to profess—but in 355 he received a grim summons to join the court at Milan. He was certainly near death; but the beautiful and, apparently, high-minded empress (a Greek) secured his acquittal and had him, to his delight, "banished," to Athens. But he was at once recalled to Milan, to learn, to his intense surprise, that he was to be made Caesar, to marry the Emperor's sister, and to take command of the armies in Gaul.

Julian was brilliantly and unexpectedly successful as a commander, and the jealousy of the easterners deepened while the hope of the pagans rose. But we have little room for history here, and we will not examine whether Julian's wife in turn was murdered while he was away in Gaul, or whether Eusebia died of a drug for removing fertility. It is enough to say that, when Constantius sought to reduce Julian's army, the legions acclaimed him emperor—his reluctance is not questioned—and Constantius died as he was making his way west to suppress the "rebellion." He would probably have failed, for the empire was as weary of him as it had become of his more distinguished father.

This was the situation in the year 361. Paganism had received a very serious blow. We shall see that Julian dared not, if he would, return to the persecution of Christianity. It was too strong. Fifty years of imperial favor and bounty had made it rich and powerful. After the record I have summarized no one will look for miracles in its advance. But we shall now see that paganism also was still too strong to be persecuted. The position of Christianity was artificial. Men—certainly far more than half the empire—clung to the old religions from conviction. The others adhered to the new from coercion or bribery. The religious fate of the world was still on the knees of the gods. Had there been a fresh series of pagan emperors, Christianity would never have become the religion of Europe.

4

The End of Paganism

Very little need be said here about the brief reign of Julian, and it is no part of our program to discuss his character. His modern biographers have entirely relieved him of the foolish and spiteful vituperation which Christian writers had fastened upon "the Apostate," and there is no historian who does not admit that even in his immaturity he exhibited a character immeasurably superior to that of his murderous and undisciplined Christian predecessors. The legend that when he was killed in Persia, two and a half years after his accession to the throne, he muttered "Thou hast conquered, Galilean"—a legend which is still sonorously declaimed from the pulpit—is a clumsy fabrication entirely inconsistent with his character. He hated and despised the religion which he had seen in action at Constantinople, but there was no element of melodrama in his attempt to check it.

Julian wrote much against Christianity, but he never persecuted it. Coercion was repugnant to his high ideals. He was a philosopher, a believer in one god whose splendor was best exhibited in the sun of southern Europe. The Christian fables were, he thought, so obviously foolish that the new converts could be reasoned out of them, and the new hypocrites would be cured by diverting the stream of gold. As far as possible, he restored the property and revenues of the temples, and he granted liberty of worship to all. The only edict of his which can be claimed as savoring of persecution is one in which he forbids Christians to teach in the higher schools of the Empire. That, however, is quite intelligible. The literature used in the schools, the Greek and Latin classics, referred from first page to last to the gods and goddesses, and we can imagine how a Christian teacher would deal with them.

On the whole, the two and a half years of Julian's reign merely checked the advance of Christianity. Pagans were displeased with him. There were many who grumbled that he seemed to wish to replace Christian mysticism and asceticism with an equally mystic and ascetic philosophy. Most of them felt that his method was too gentle and ethereal for the age. The implement of the religious teacher had come to be recognized as the scourge, and Julian would not wield it. He disliked the brutal games of the Amphitheater as much as he disliked nightingale's tongues and Cyprian wine and nude Syrian dancing girls. He trusted time; and time brought his ruthless scythe into play in the third year of the young philosopher's reign.

The troops selected a popular commander, Jovian, to succeed Julian, but he died in a few months, and another popular general, Valentinian, was elected. Both were Christians. Julian had not surrounded himself with hypocrites and adventurers by granting promotion to those who exchanged the worship of Christ for the worship of Sol. He had chosen good soldiers and had worked for the Empire. Only on one occasion had he shown some feeling, and Christian writers do not fail to exaggerate his conduct. Valentinian had assisted, as an officer of the body-guard, at a pagan ceremony, and, when the priest had, in sprinkling the people with holy water—a custom taken over by the Church—let a few drops fall on his uniform, he had there and then struck the priest on the face. One can imagine what a Catholic monarch would do if a Protestant officer of his guard even today did such a thing. Julian nominally banished him, but apparently merely removed him from the guard.

But Valentinian was shrewd, and the story of his reign need not be told here. He made his brother Valens co-Emperor, and they both preserved a complete neutrality in regard to religion. There was complete liberty for all cults, in fact favor for all: which satisifed the pagans and greatly angered the Christian minority. Their formula was, as one of their greatest writers naively puts it: No liberty for error—that is to say, for any person's opinion but your own. Valens was an Arian, Valentinian a Trinitarian; and the pagans probably enjoyed the difference over a diphthong as much as Gibbon does. Moreover, Valentinian, the orthodox, had a will of his own. He quite clearly took a second wife (see my *Empresses of Rome*) when the first failed to satisfy his violent temperament, and the clergy were as meekly silent about his long adultery as about his brutalities. Neither Christian court recommended the new religion more attractively than the court of Constans or Constantius had done.

Thus by 375, when Valentinian died—bursting a blood vessel in one of his fierce bursts of rage—the religious issue was as undecided as ever. Sixty-four years of imperial favor had, of course, led to a very considerable growth of Christianity. In the east, especially, most of the temples had been closed for twenty years, and their revenues destroyed. Few religions would survive that blow alone. If all the churches of America were closed for twenty years, and the clerical income entirely suspended. . . . At all events, let these plain historical facts be realized by those who talk rhetorically about the triumph of Christianity. It would still be ten years before the Christians of Antioch numbered one-fifth of the population, and by that time the persecution of the pagans was again in full blast. Christianity had no more appeal than any other new religion.

Gratian, a youth of sixteen, succeeded his father Valentinian in the west. Valens died in 378 and Gratian chose a seasoned commander, Theodosius, to take the purple in the eastern empire. It was this pair, an immature youth of weak character and an ignorant soldier of strong character, who came fully under the influence of the priests and established Christianity in Europe. For some time the arrogance of bishops had increased with the superstition of their nominal rulers. Now a formidable priest, St. Ambrose, came upon the scene. Paul had founded the religion of Jesus. Ambrose established it.

Ambrose, an ex-Prefect of the Roman Empire, with legal training, had become bishop of Milan the year before Gratian ascended the throne in that city: for Rome had been deserted by the Christian emperors. It is said that Gratian at once refused the title of Sovereign Pontiff of the old religion, which was still the state-religion, but the date is uncertain. What is certain is that Gratian had his father raised to the rank of the gods, in the pagan manner, and in 378 he decreed liberty of all cults. Ambrose was, however, subtly gaining control of him, and in 382 the pagan world seethed with excitement. Gratian confiscated the revenues and property of the temples, annulled all the privileges of the priests and Vestal Virgins, and commanded that the Altar of Victory, the type and emblem of the established Roman religion, should be removed from the Senate House in Rome. "Thou hast gratified me," says Ambrose in a letter (Ep. II) to Gratian, "by restoring peace to the Church and shutting the mouths of its enemies." Gratian had also gratified another bishop, Pope Damasus of Rome.

One smiles at the "peace" which Gratian had "restored"; but Ambrose—the reader may have read about his zeal for "discovering" relics—ceased to use the precise language of a lawyer when he became a bishop. He told Gratian that the majority of the Senators at Rome were Christians, and that the custom of offering incense to Jupiter before this Altar of Victory hurt their consciences. It happens that St. Augustine came to Rome from Africa just at that time, and he tells us that "nearly the whole of the Roman nobles" were pagans (*Confessions*, VIII, 2). We know quite well from the Letters of Symmachus (the Prefect) and the *Saturnalia* of Macrobius that that was true. Very few male members of noble Roman families had deserted the old religion.

I may say that the modern successors of Ambrose and Damasus still repeat the statement that the majority of the patricians were Christians, although I have over and over again pointed to the decisive passage which I discovered in Augustine's *Confessions*. "The world wishes to be deceived," says an old Latin proverb. Substitute "the clergy" for "the world."

Gratian, however, was murdered in one of the endless provincial revolts in 383, and his young brother Valentinian II succeeded him. The mother was an Arian, and for a time it seemed that the influence of Ambrose would be checked. But a new age had set in. Ambrose and his flock defied even the imperial troops, hurled the epithet Jezebel at the empress, and, when a usurper pressed her and her son, and she appealed to Theodosius in the east, she was, for her "heresy," almost allowed to perish, though Theodosius owed his throne to her and her son. The price of his aid was, however, the return to orthodoxy of the boy-emperor, and Ambrose now ruled the world through Theodosius and the child.

It cannot be said that even now Providence had shown much discrimination in the choice of its instruments. Against Ambrose, a typical zealous priest, I urge nothing except his readiness (as seen in his manufacture of relics and martyrs) to admit that the end justifies the means. About Pope Damasus I shall have much to say in the next chapter. But Theodosius was the chief instrument in the imposition upon the world of the new religion, and even the most lenient of modern historians gives him a streak of savagery.

A notorious historical incident, which recalls the semi-savagery of Constantine and Valentinian, and almost rivals the insane rage of Nero, had sufficed of itself to prevent the Church from giving a halo to its great benefactor. His panegyrists praise his leniency in "pardoning" the citizens of Antioch for a revolt. So utterly detested had he become that a mob tore down the statues of himself and his family and trampled the fragments in the mire. In a fit of anger he degraded the city to the status of a village, closed all its places of entertainment, cut off its food supply, extorted by torture a series of charges against leading men, executed them and pauperized their families; but when the fit of temper was over, and the graves covered, he "pardoned" Antioch.

Thessalonica next outraged his majesty, in 390, and some of his officers were murdered by the mob. He sent an army of barbaric mercenaries to avenge the insult, with orders to invite the people treacherously to games in the Circus and then massacre all that it contained. No Turk ever committed so foul an outrage in those parts. Many thousands—the estimates vary from 7,000 to 150,000—of men, women, and children were slain by the soldiers. So ghastly was the deed, so just the irony of the pagans, that St. Ambrose compelled the monarch of the Roman world to do penance for it. If we believe the pagan writer Zosimus, Theodosius often varied his hard campaigns and his spells of devotion with these bursts of ungovernable fury or weeks of sensual indulgence. But he had one master, Ambrose. The monks and people of a small town in Persia burned the Jewish synagogue, and the prefect justly ordered them to rebuild it. Theodosius confirmed the order. But Ambrose violently compelled him to withdraw, and monks and people in the east gaily set out to finish the work begun by Constantius.

Through this man and the boy-emperor (or his mother)

in Italy the bishops now entered upon the final campaign against paganism. It is at this date that the word "pagan" (the Latin word for "villager" or rustic) was first applied by the Christians; at a time when Rome and Antioch were still overwhelmingly pagan. We have the invaluable testimony of Augustine, who was not yet a Christian, for Rome. In the year 385 he saw the wild procession through the streets, while all Rome looked on, of the priests of Cybele. All the temples of the Roman religion were as active as ever; and we know from St. Jerome that the Manicheans and followers of other Asiatic religions were as conspicuous as ever. Christianity still had no more hope of "converting" the world than Roman Catholicism has today of converting France, England, or the United States. The condition of the Church in Rome was sordid (as we shall see), and very few Romans of distinction (of the male sex) would associate with it.

I am not sure that even Theodosius and his successors would have scourged the reluctant world into the new religion, but an event was now preparing which was in any case destined to revolutionize the history of Europe. We interpret history today, not by fables and miracles, but by economic facts. And just at the time when the Roman Empire was distracted and enfeebled by this bitter quarrel about Jupiter and Jesus, there occurred in the northeast something which was to strain the old civilization to the utmost. Drought and famine on the plains of Asia drove an immense army of fierce nomads, the Huns, into Europe. This terror drove the half-Romanized barbarians of Europe upon the Empire, and, bled by seven centuries of wars, weakened by five centuries of economic parasitism, diverted from its national problems by the new religion, European civilization blindly waited for its doom.

There is no need to dwell at great length on the more effective persecution of paganism—that is to say, of all religions except the Christian and all sects except the orthodox—which now followed. So far is it from true that the battle had been won that in 384 the Romans tried once more to get back the Altar of Victory. The Prefect of Rome, Symmachus, an eloquent orator, headed a delegation to Milan. Ambrose artfully procured that he should be directed to send in advance a copy of his oration; and Ambrose's reply was ready. Candidly, Ambrose won. Who could make a convincing defense of gods and goddesses in whom he did not literally believe? It was time they went.

But what Ambrose said and did is interesting. We have his letters to the boy-emperor. "Do not let anybody impose on thy youth," he naively says; and he cunningly reminds him that his throne depends on the zealous Theodosis, who is suppressing paganism in the east. It is his argument, however, that I have recommended most strongly to modern apologists. It is—Evolution! Nothing is fixed and stable, he says. Day succeeds night: spring succeeds winter. The law is change and progress. So in religion, when creeds are plainly old and outworn—it is a fine piece of Rationalism.

The altar was not restored, but Valentinian in turn was murdered a few years later. A pagan, Eugenius, was put on the throne (392–394), and it seemed that Jupiter had at last awakened. Theodosius, of course, came over and made an end of him, but he died a few months later, and the bishops got their golden opportunity: two boy-emperors, Honorius (aged seven) in the west and Arcadius (aged fourteen) in the east.

Theodosius had issued a series of decrees like those of Constantius. He had begun in 381, with a cruel enactment that no man who reverted from Christianity to paganism could make a valid will. This astute piece of priestcraft, which made wife and family the tearful guardians of a man's religion, was adopted throughout the Empire; yet there was so much "apostasy" that Theodosius had to repeat it in 383 and 391. In the last year reverts were declared "infamous." In 386 Theodosius sent a zealous envoy to close the august temples of Egypt, where Greek and Egyptian cults still flourished. Under the protection of his soldiers the fanatical monks and priests led their followers to storm the rival places of worship, and requisite buildings and statues were soon in ruins. The magnificent temple, or group of buildings, in honor of Serapis at Alexandria was leveled to the ground under the lead of the archbishop—a man with the character as well as the zeal of a Vandal—and the great Library was plundered and an invaluable ancient literature destroyed. The flame spread to Syria, where Bishop Marcellus led his mobs, with a sprinkling of soldiers and gladiators, to the destruction of the most beautiful temples. In faraway Gaul St. Martin of Tours led the ragged regiments. In Carthage and other less insane localities the great temples were converted into churches.

But there was still an obstinate pagan reluctance to perceive the beauty of the new religion, and Theodosius continued to fulminate from the palace of Neronian luxury, where he was enthroned amidst a crowd of repulsive eunuchs, hysterical women, and scheming priests. In 391 it was decreed, both for east and west:

> Let none befoul himself with sacrifices, or offer innocent victims [mainly incense], or enter the temples, or defend statues made by human hand, lest he become guilty in the eyes of both human and divine law.

Several local decrees enforced this, and before the end of the same year Theodosius enacted that the penalty of disobedience should be death. He repeated this in the following year, and imposed a sentence of confiscation for minor acts of worship.

Next year, as I said, Theodosius died, and in the west at least the pagans had a respite. In the east, where sixty years of almost continuous persecution of the pagans and imperial patronage of Christians had made the Church a formidable body, if not the majority, the doom of the old religions was sealed. Most of the temples were wrecked, and the pagans, at first sullenly, took their superstitions and whatever vices they had to the new conventicles across the street. St. John Chrysostom tells us in one of his sermons that many amongst his "hundred thousand" did not even believe in the resurrection. But the Church was rapidly adopting the operatic rites to which they were accustomed—incense, holy water, etc.—Mary was replacing Cybele and Isis, and "'statues made by human hand," which the emperor had scornfully proscribed, were being copied from the old cults and were giving a familiar appearance to the new temples.

In the west paganism died hard. Childish as its mythology was, it took Christianity nearly a hundred years of use of the imperial resources and fifty years of persecution to destroy it. At the death of the fanatical Theodosius a sober statesman, Stilicho, a Christian, but sensible of the grave condition of the Empire, ruled in the name of the boy-emperors. Bishops blessed the heredity principle so foreign to Roman law, now that it favored them, as they found it convenient to have youthful "rulers"— with mothers. But Stilicho resisted their frantic appeals, and the pagans remained free and, I believe, in the majority until the statesman was murdered in 408.

Now, through the young emperor, the hand of the bishops gave the rival religions their death-blow. It was the period when pathetic stories of the martyrs were being fabricated, and the Christian world was still reading the rhetorical and inaccurate work of Lactantius, *On the Deaths of the Persecutors.* But that was another matter. It was an equal sin to persecute truth and to spare error. Honorius decreed that the last revenues of the temples should be confiscated, the last statues and altars should be destroyed, and the last temples should be converted to public uses. Bishops were now empowered to see that the law was enforced and any magistrate whom they denounced for remissness was to be punished with the enormous fine of twenty gold pounds, or about $5,000.

The bishops "saw to it," as they were enjoined to do, but a larger providence than theirs was governing the affairs of Italy. Alaric and his terrible Goths were even then making for Rome, and in 410 the world shuddered to hear of the fall of the mighty city. The Christian emperor had fled, and the pagans had an hour of freedom. But the story of Rome was over. Its most faithful sons had died resisting the invaders. Its pacifists had become Christian priests, surviving the ruin. The wealth, even the families, of its patricians, were scattered. In name the empire lingered on for a time, but it was lifeless. Fresh sentences of death issued from the imperial-clerical arsenal, the schools—the last refuge of the gods—were closed, the doors of the great Roman temples were sealed and the fabrics allowed to decay. Paganism, when it went down to Hades, took civilization with it.

For years afterward we find pagans in the provinces and in high positions in the army and state. It is believed by historians that the great jurists who drew up the Justinian Code were secret pagans. St. Augustine informs us of much paganism in Roman Africa, both amongst the people and the educated, until in 428 the Vandals crossed the Straits of Gibraltar and trampled under foot the last province of the great empire. But we need not follow the final flickers of paganism. We have seen how Europe was "persuaded" to embrace the gentle religion of the prophet of Nazareth.

Let me repeat to any religious reader that this is no disputed or poorly authenticated story that I have laid before him. The Edicts I have quoted or summarized may be read today in the Theodosian Code—if you read Latin, for clerical writers do not care to translate them. The facts were, in the main, given by Gibbon, more than a century ago, and where he errs, he errs in liberality to the Church. Count Beugnot's *Histoire de la destruction du paganisme* and Professor Schultze's *Geschichte des Untergangs des griechisch-römischen Heidentum* give all the fcts I have given. Of more recent works Boissier's *Fin du paganisme* and Ferrero's *Ruin of Ancient Civilization* entirely agree, though they are concerned mainly with other aspects. There is in this booklet, startling as it may seem, not one word of disputed history except a few such incidental matters as the guilt for various murders. Some day I trust to write the story in full of that historic struggle. Here I must close with a brief sketch of the results.

5

The Glorious Result

Christianity had triumphed. With the imperial hammer it had leveled the temples, with imperial gold it had built new churches, and with the imperial spear it had driven what was left of the Roman people into them. Few Christian leaders had hesitated. For a time, when the force of his pagan ideals was still in his blood, St. Augustine had wondered whether coercion was either just or religious. But with the advance of his deterioration he penned his famous "Compelle intrare" ("Compel them to come in"), making the excuse, not merely that these were the words of Jesus in a parable, but that the *efficacy* of the new method had persuaded him to agree. The end justified the means. He was still uneasy, however, until he found a new formula: "What worse death of the soul can there be than liberty to err?" Orthodoxy is my doxy: heterodoxy is yours.

Had paganism, you may ask, a glorious body of martyrs to compare with the Christian? No man knows how many Mithraists or Manichaeans died. The survivor in the struggle, Christianity, naturally did not keep records of its dead rivals. As to the old Roman and Greek and Eygptian religions, we must remember two things. First, they were not exclusive. A believer in Jupiter did not say that the gods of other folk were devils to whom it would be dishonorable to offer a few grains of incense. Secondly, there was in the Roman religion no priesthood corresponding to the Christian. The priests were civilians. The religion was part of the life of the state. The last thing its priests would dream of doing was to preach sermons or threaten a man with damnation for not accepting a formula.

And there also, you have the essential difference between Roman and Christian persecution. Rome did not say: This is the truth, and we compel you to subscribe to it. It said: Religion is a part of the corporate or social life, and you shall have no "private gods." It was wrong, and educated Romans knew it. The old law was applied, as we saw, for social reasons. The Christians, they said, were secretive, anti-national, intolerant, disrespectful to the emperor and the law, dangerous to the state in recommending abstention. Still, from the modern point of view, they were wrong. But far more wrong and poisonous is the idea that you certainly possess the eternal truth and can put a knife at your neighbor's breast and make him accept it.

How many Americans who are amiable to Rome and resent these rude criticisms of mine know that, as we shall see, that is the law of the Roman Catholic Church today? It is bound by its actual law to have me burned at the stake if any government will oblige it.

What was the effect of introducing this ghastly principle of coercion of opinion and laying the foundation for the horrors of the Middle Ages? There are two parts to the thesis which you hear in sermons. The triumph was spiritual: the result was moral. And the second part is as demonstrably false as the first.

Dean Milman in his *History of Latin Christianity* frankly described the fearful degeneration of Europe after 420, when we may date the full triumph of Christianity. No one disputes it. The world passed rapidly into a state of semi-barbarism. But, you may say, this change of religion coincided with the destruction of civilization by the barbarians from the north. Yes, I allow for it in other books, in which I expose the appalling fallacy of the claims that Christianity gave the world education, freed the slave, uplifted woman, and created modern civilization. But the writers who so insistently urge this point against me forget, or do not know, that one half the Roman Empire, the eastern half, never fell to the barbarians, yet it became as corrupt and vicious, and almost as ignorant as Europe.

Let me give a curious little illustration. Some years ago I wrote for a certain publisher the *Empresses of Rome* to which I have referred. It did not please him. It was not picturesque enough. There were too many good women, too few Messalinas, in it. Until Christian empresses appeared, the consort of the Roman emperor was, during two hundred and fifty out of the three hundred years, a good woman. This was not interesting, in spite of the last few chapters on the lively ladies of the Christian courts. So I wrote a continuation, the *Empresses of Constantinople,* all of whom were Christians. That was a spicy story.

Here I propose only to give a few authentic details about the progress of morals in the Roman Empire during the fourth century when the new religion was spreading. We have had some glimpses of life in the various palaces. Not very edifying, were they? Greasy eunuchs, hired murderers, bears fed on human victims (in Valentinian's palace), pederasty, luxury, bursts of rage. . . . A one-sided story, you may say. I challenge you to find in any history of the fourth century a single Christian emperor who even approaches the standard of "Julian the Apostate." His chief defect was that he was too virtuous.

Sir Samuel Dill has written the finest and most scholarly picture of life in the fourth and fifth centuries (*Roman Society in the Last Centuries of the Western Empire*). He is, I believe, a Protestant, and, while he frankly redeems the pagans from the calumnies which ignorant religious writers have put on them, showing that they lived and died like gentlemen, he tells only such virtues and attractions as he can find in the Christian side. Mr. Lecky (*History of European Morals*), though a Rationalist, was just as eager to say the best that any historian could for Christianity. And when he has said it, he writes:

> After every legitimate allowance has been made, the pictures of Roman society by Ammianus Marcellinus, of the society of Marseilles by Salvian [a priest], of the society of Asia Minor and of Constantinople by Chrysostom [a bishop], as well as the whole tenor of the history, and innumerable incidental notices in the writers of the time, exhibit a condition of depravity, and especially of degradation, which has seldom been surpassed. The corruption had reached classes and institutions that appeared the most holy. The *agapae,* or love-feasts, which formed one of the most touching symbols of Christian unity, had become scenes of drunkenness and of riot. . . . The commemoration of the martyrs soon degenerated into scandalous dissipation. Fairs were held on the occasion, gross breaches of chastity were frequent, and the annual festival was suppressed on account of the immortality it produced. The ambiguous position of the clergy with reference to marriage already led to grave disorder. In the time of St. Cyprian, before the outbreak of the Decian persecution, it had been common to find clergy professing celibacy, but keeping, under various pretexts, their mistresses in their houses; and, after Constantine, the complaints on this subject became loud and general. Virgins and monks often lived together in the same house, professing sometimes to share in chastity the same bed. Rich widows were surrounded by swarms of clerical sycophants who addressed them in tender diminutives. . . . Noble ladies, pretending a desire to lead a higher life, abandoned their husbands to live with low-born slaves. Palestine, which was soon crowded with pilgrims, had

become, in the time of St. Gregory of Nyssa [fourth century], a hot-bed of debauchery. . . . The luxury and ambition of the higher prelates, and the passion for amusement of the inferior priests, were bitterly acknowledged. In the lay world, perhaps, the chief characteristic was extreme childishness. . . . The level of public men was extremely depressed. . . . There existed a combination of vice and superstition which is eminently prejudicial to the nobility, though not equally detrimental to the happiness, of man. Public opinion was so low that very many forms of vice attracted little condemnation and punishment, while undoubting belief in the efficacy of superstitious rites claimed the imagination and allayed the terrors of conscience. There was more falsehood and treachery than under the Caesars. . . . (1911 ed., II, 64–5).

This is the verdict of the "gentle Lecky" who has paid Christianity more undeserved compliments than any other historian. In ample footnotes he gives the authorities, but it would be enough to read the sermons in which the Christian Fathers describe their new flocks. St. Augustine tells us how St. Ambrose in Milan had to suppress the "love-feasts" (in the churches) because of the orgies which attended them. But I will add two little pictures to the broad account given by Lecky.

Very few Roman bishops had the least distinction to catch the eye of the world, until, about the middle of the fourth century, one of them weakly signed an heretical formula and split his people into two parties. The bishopric was now rich. Forty years of imperial bounty had fattened it. Men felt that it was worth fighting for, and, to the intense amusement of the pagans, they fought. After one "election meeting" in a church, in October 366, the "ushers" picked up from the floor one hundred and sixty Christian corpses! It is sheer affectation of modern Roman Catholic writers to question this, as we learn it from a report to the emperor by two priests of the time. The sanguinary riots of the Christians which filled the streets of Rome with blood for a week, are, in fact, ironically recorded by the contemporary Roman writer, Ammianus Marcellinus.

In one day the Christians murdered more of their brethren than the pagans can be positively proved to have martyred in three centuries, and the total number of the slain during the fight for the papal chair is probably as great as the total number of actual martyrs. If we add to these the number of the slain in the fights of Arians and Trinitarians in th east and the fights of Catholics and Donatists in Africa, we get a sum of "martyrs" many times as large as the genuine victims of Roman law; and we should still have to add the massacre by Theodosius at Thessalonica, the massacre of a regiment of Arian soldiers, the lives sacrificed under Constantius, Valentinian, etc.

This frightful and sordid temper of the new Christendom is luridly exhibited in the murder of Hypatia of Alexandria in 415. Under the "great" Father of the Church, Cyril of Alexandria, the Christian mob became so imbued with the beautiful counsels of the Sermon the Mount that, led by a minor cleric of the church, it stripped Hypatia naked, gashed her with oyster shells until she died, and burned her remains. She was not, as modern writers (misled by Kingsley's novel) persist in saying, a young woman, but, as I have shown by research in the Greek writers of the time, a woman of advanced age (probably about sixty), of the highest ideals and character, and of remarkable knowledge and ability. This barbaric fury raged from Rome to Alexandria and Antioch, and degraded the cities with spectacles that paganism had never witnessed.

The common Christian boast is that at least the new religion made the world chaste. I would rather have the scarlet sins of Paphos or of the groves of Antioch than the red hate and brutality which succeeded them; but, in point of fact, there was no change whatever in sex-morals.

Religious writers have a stock selection of quotations from the letters of St. Jerome which show that he had a small nursery of virtue and asceticism in the noble mansions of Rome where, the preacher generally adds, vice had hitherto been supreme. The letters of the contemporary pagan Symmachus sufficiently refute the last part of this statement; but what is more interesting is that these very letters of St. Jerome, from which a few examples of virtue were culled long ago and are handed on from one religious writer to another, are the most damning indictment of the sex-morals of the new Christian world that any man could pen.

Jerome's friend Pope Damasus, whose supporters had, as we have seen, literally cut his way, with swords and axes, to the papal chair through the supporters of the rival candidate Ursicinus, has been "sainted" by his Church. Never did the halo sit more incongruously! His nickname amongst the clergy was *matronarum auriscalpius* ("tickler of matron's ears"), and the Christian authorities were obliged to pass a law making invalid bequests to the monks and clergy. His priests were so habitually immoral that Jerome, in the much-quoted letters, sternly warns his "daughters" to beware of them. They must never remain in the same room with a Roman priest, he says. If you admire at least *his* delicacy, let me quote his advice to a refined maiden of noble birth when she finds herself in the same room with a priest. "At least let some necessity of the bladder or the . . . compel thee to leave the room." The modern police would be interested if I literally translated the word I have left blank. He tells his virgins, and us, that elderly and wealthy widows of the church have young priests as lovers, that priests have mistresses in their homes, that nearly all the priests are constantly bent on seduction, that large numbers enter the clergy precisely because of the golden opportunities of sex indulgence, that most of the so-called virgins of the church are hypocrites, and so on. He himself was, of course, accused of secret relations with one of his ascetic pupils, the wealthy and beautiful Paula; but I am quite prepared to believe his word that he had long since (probably for very effective reasons as well as from piety) retired from immorality.

In short, repugnant as we may find the older spectacle of educated Roman gentlemen inspecting the entrails of birds to take the omens, it was far less repulsive than the spectacle mercilessly depicted for us by Jerome, who lived many years in Rome. Religious people are grossly deceived by the pictures of ancient virtue which are put before them. A dozen or so women of the patrician class at Rome are glowingly described as models of virtue and self-sacrifice, but no religious writer would dare to publish in full the letters of St. Jerome from which these few examples of virtue are taken. Jerome frankly describes his small group of pupils as a few just women in a world of corruption. Nor is it truthful to represent the educated people or aristocracy of Rome as having accepted the faith because a few mansions on the Aventine Hill are open to the clergy. "The Church of God is made up of the lowest people," Jerome bitterly complains. Rome changed its professions of faith only, not its ways.

And this was only the beginning. This was the fourth century. The fifth was worse, the sixth far worse, the succeeding centuries increasingly worse. The great Roman system of education was, as we shall see, completely destroyed, and all Europe passed into a condition of complete illiteracy and dense ignorance in which vice and violence were only surpassed by superstition. Salvianus, a priest of Marseilles of the fifth century, deplores the vanished virtue of the pagan world and declares that "The whole body of Christians is a sink of iniquity." "Very few," he says, "avoid evil." He challenges his readers: "How many in the Church will you find that are not drunkards or adulterers, or fornicators, or gamblers, or robbers, or murderers—or all together?" (*De Gubernatione Dei*, III,

9). Gregory of Tours, in the next century, gives, incredible as it may seem, an even darker picture of the Christian world, over part of which he presides. You cannot read these truths, unless you can read bad Latin, because they are never translated. It is the flowers, the rare examples of virtue, the untruths of Eusebius and the Martyrologies, that are translated. It is the legends of St. Agnes and St. Catherine, the heroic fictions of St. Lawrence and St. Sebastian that you read. But there were ten vices for every virtue, ten lies for every truth, a hundred murders for every genuine martyrdom.

The Church had triumphed; and humanity fell deeply in the sordid yet fascinating Middle Ages. The doctrines of the Church were shaped amidst the growing passion-lit darkness of the time, and the Papacy won its supremacy and power. It is untrue that the new religion strengthened the passion and protected the virtue of women: it is an untruth as humorously remote from the fact as is possible. But hardly less fantastic are the claims that Christianity emancipated the slave and gave education to the worker. The world gained nothing by the enforcement upon it of the new religion. Did it lose? We must examine carefully every aspect of the human need before we venture to answer this.